Outdoor Adventures with Children

Lake District

About the Authors

Rachel Crolla and Carl McKeating live at the edge of the Yorkshire Dales with their two young adventurers. They have visited the Lake District on family holidays since their own childhoods and have fond memories of being taken on some of the routes in this book. They are both passionate about passing on their love and respect of outdoor environments to a new generation. Rachel and Carl are outdoors writers and photographers who have hiked, scrambled and climbed all over Europe, exploring the major mountain ranges. They also enjoy cycling. In 2007, Rachel became the first woman to climb to the highest point of every country in Europe. The couple's resulting guidebook, *Europe's High Points*, was published by Cicerone in 2009. The couple have since worked on guides to Snowdonia, France and Northern England. When they are not having outdoor adventures, Carl is working on his doctorate about Mont Blanc and Rachel is a teacher.

Other Cicerone guides by the authors

Europe's High Points
Walking in the Auvergne
Scrambles in Snowdonia (updated by the authors)
Cycling the Way of the Roses (Rachel Crolla)

Outdoor adventures with children
Lake District

40 family days with under 12s exploring,
biking, scrambling, on the water and more

by Rachel Crolla and Carl McKeating

Juniper House, Murley Moss,
Oxenholme Road, Kendal, Cumbria LA9 7RL
www.cicerone.co.uk

© Rachel Crolla and
Carl McKeating 2019
First edition 2019
ISBN: 978 1 85284 956 6

Printed by KHL Printing, Singapore
A catalogue record for this book is
available from the British Library.

© Crown copyright 2019
OS PU100012932

All photographs are by the authors
unless otherwise stated.

Updates to this guide

While every effort is made by our authors
to ensure the accuracy of guidebooks
as they go to print, changes can occur
during the lifetime of an edition. Any
updates that we know of for this guide will
be on the Cicerone website
(www.cicerone.co.uk/956/updates), so
please check before planning your trip.
We also advise that you check information
about such things as transport,
accommodation and shops locally. Even
rights of way can be altered over time. We
are always grateful for information about
any discrepancies between a guidebook
and the facts on the ground, sent by email
to updates@cicerone.co.uk or by post to
Cicerone, Juniper House, Murley Moss,
Oxenholme Road, Kendal, LA9 7RL.

Register your book: To sign up to receive
free updates, special offers and GPX files
where available, register your book at
www.cicerone.co.uk.

*Front cover: Striding down the flanks
of Loughrigg, high above Grasmere
(Adventure 7)*

*Half title: There is always plenty to find on
the beach at Maryport (Adventure 38)*

Acknowledgments

This book has been in the pipeline
for a long time. Born from the love of
the outdoors that was kindled in us as
children and that we wished to pass on
to our own and other children, it has only
come to fruition thanks to the invaluable
help and support of many people.
Thanks in particular to Joe, Jonathan
and Lesley Williams and the team at
Cicerone for believing that this project
was worthwhile.

It has been our pleasure and privilege
to go out adventuring with some keen
members of the next generation of
outdoor enthusiasts. Thanks in particular
go to Julija Moskalina, Ayrton and Lydia;
the Hatch family; Dave, Sally, Heidi and
Lucy Emery; Mark, Sam and Luke Barrett;
Dougie and Robbie Thistlethwaite and
family; Natty, Rafferty and Monty Truss
and family; Ben and Emily Ward and
family; Robert and Olly Brooks and
family; the Hartley family; Jonah Brittain.
We are grateful to all the families who
gave permission for photographs of
their children to appear in this book.
Also thanks to Dennis Mayho and the
Robinson family for their route ideas.
Special thanks to Stephanie Crolla for
providing 'base camp' at her caravan in
the Lake District.

Final thanks go to our intrepid explorers,
Heather and Rosa, who have been willing
'guinea pigs' testing out these routes
come rain or shine. Their smiles and
enthusiasm have coloured countless
memorable Lakeland family adventures
and ensured this book has been terrific
fun to write.

Contents

List of adventures

Safety notice and disclaimer

This guidebook has been prepared in good faith to help parents who are taking children on adventures in the outdoors.

Developing your child's abilities, knowledge and experience is something that should not be forced or rushed. The aim is to give you ideas to help your child discover and develop a love of the outdoors, which will last a lifetime, and to ensure that your child has a great time, safely.

As a parent you are responsible for judging the capabilities of your child. The notes under the How to use this guide and grading section give information about the capabilities your child will need to be able to manage each activity. This can only be indicative – every child and every situation is different, so it is important to make continuous judgments, even after you have started out, and to be prepared to turn back if the situation changes.

Make sure you understand the route or activity you are doing before setting off. Read the guide carefully. Always have a map and other navigational aids (compass or GPS) with you and know how use them. Check weather and hill conditions before you start and be prepared to turn back if conditions change.

Always have ample warm clothing, for your child and yourself, as well as good quality waterproofs. Strenuous activities burn a lot of energy, so be sure to take sufficient food and drinks for all the party. Children will often run out of energy very quickly unless they eat regularly.

Be aware of the safety issues for the activity you are doing. This book gives general guidance, but you are expected to understand the risks and safety issues around water, cycling, hillwalking and scrambling and take the appropriate gear and safety equipment in each case.

As well as knowing your child's capabilities, it is important to know your own. Do not undertake activities outside – or anywhere approaching the limits of – your own comfort zone. If in doubt, do something easier, or develop your skills before venturing into the outdoors with your children. **Please read the Introduction for important safety information and tips.**

The author and publisher have made every effort to ensure that the information contained in this guide was correct when it went to press, but, except for any liability that cannot be excluded by law, they cannot accept responsibility for any loss, injury or inconvenience sustained by any person using this book.

Route symbols on OS map extracts

 green route   green alternative route/extension

 blue route   blue alternative route/extension

 red route   red alternative route/extension

 black route   black alternative route/extension

(SF) start/finish point   **(F)** finish point

(S) start point   **(SF)** alternative start/finish point

> route direction   **for OS legend see printed OS maps**

Activity symbol key

🚶 Hiking   ⛵ Boating

🚴 Cycling   🧗 Scrambling

🏊 On the water   ⛰ Mountain Climb

🏃 Exploring   🏕 Overnight Stay

Scrambling to a look-out on Wild Cat Island (Adventure 1)

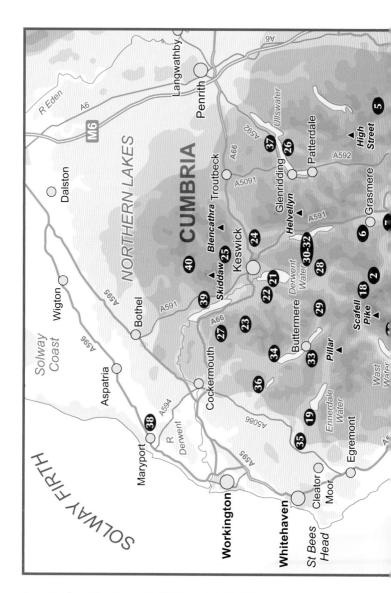

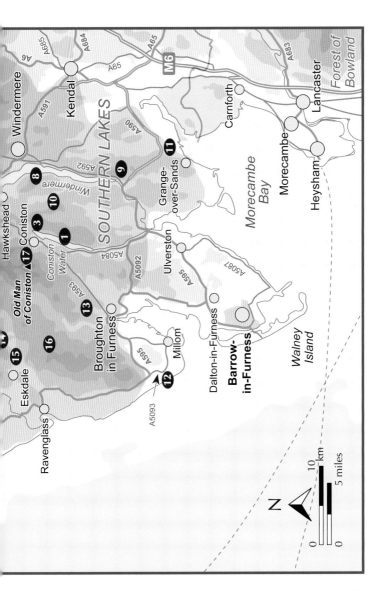

Whitewater Dash from the track to Skiddaw House (Adventure 40)

Making this guide

After years of having outdoor adventures on our own terms, when we became parents our focus shifted to include our children and pass on a love of wild places to them. Like most aspects of parenting, this is a learning process not without its occasional ups and downs. Yet in spite of a few lost mittens and soggy picnics, our children have genuinely loved their outings and inspired us to see the outdoors with fresh eyes.

Children find joy and adventure in every stick, pebble and creepy crawly they discover along the way. This enthusiasm is infectious. Yes, we've had to slow down on our family adventures, but that has led us to do things we may well have otherwise ignored: skimming stones on pebbly beaches, climbing trees, flying kites and finding geocaches. Watching our children grow from tottering toddlers into young people who appreciate the beauty of nature and understand the importance of looking after it, we have shared their pride in pushing themselves to climb mountains, learn to ride bikes and brave the chilly Lakeland waters.

Time and again our children have surprised us with what they can achieve with support and encouragement (and perhaps the occasional bit of good old-fashioned 'get to the top of this bit and there'll be a sweet stop' bribery!).

As all parents know, children are full of surprises. Our eldest set off on a walk around Buttermere when she was nearly three. After 200m she wanted to be carried. We distracted her from this request. Thereafter she ambled happily around the whole of the lake without a single moan – exceeding all our expectations. Three years later, and at a similar age, our youngest gave us the same sort of surprise by managing the hikes to Skiddaw House and to Mosedale Bothy with relative ease. Likewise we have been impressed by the determination of friends' children to manage things that are fairly tough adventures for reasonably fit adults, and yet do so while having a great deal of fun – an 8-year-old zipping round the Quercus Trail, 9 and 11-year-old brothers being full of beans on Scafell Pike, 4-year-old friends clambering their way up Catbells while looking for 'cats' and 'Mrs Tiggy-Winkle's house' – these are just a few of the many examples we could give.

Overall, making this guide has emphasised the value of a break from the relentless digital world and the pressures of modern living, and made us feel that a back-to-basics outdoor adventure cannot be beaten!

Rachel and Carl

Enjoying the art of scrambling on Cathells (Adventure 22)

Introduction

Full of beans on the way up Loughrigg (Adventure 7)

The Lake District with children

Twinkling tarns for skimming stones and craggy summits for scrambling – the Lake District is a natural adventure playground for children of all ages. The remarkable beauty of Lakeland is no secret, but the magical combination of sparkling waters and steep mountainsides will capture not only adults' imaginations but those of children too. It is the perfect place to share outdoor adventures with your family, have fun together and inspire the next generation to love and cherish wild and rural landscapes. Spend the night in a remote mountain bothy, take a dip in a hidden pool, feel the freedom of cycling on a forest bridleway or scramble up high on rocky peaks – the Lake District is full of opportunities for unforgettable family adventures.

This book suggests 40 adventure routes for the family. They give a combination of many activities that will spark the interest of both children and adults: hiking, biking, scrambling, boating and swimming. While there are some more traditional routes, all are more than 'just' a walk and can be presented to reluctant participants as 'finding a secret cave' or 'climbing to a hilltop fort'. Whereas there have been previous guides to children's walks (often flat, pushchair friendly and fairly unadventurous), the logic of this first multi-activity guide is that many families prefer to enjoy a mixture of outdoor pursuits on holiday and do something exciting together.

The routes chosen for this guide have all been rigorously road-tested and have got the thumbs up from those harshest of critics – the under-12s. All the route descriptions are written with families of all ages in mind. They provide clear information about what to expect, with the aim of giving adults a sense of what adventures will best suit their children's capabilities.

This guide is designed for long-term use as your children grow up. There are shorter options with idyllic paddling, caves, castles and picnicking spots for younger children and more demanding alternatives such as backpacking on Skiddaw, mountain biking in the Whinlatter Forest, completing Ullswater's four island boating challenge or even scaling the heights of England's highest peak, Scafell Pike, by a lesser known flank. The routes are spread out through most of the major lakes and valleys of the national park. Some include well-known beauty spots such as on the Tarn Hows geocaching trail or the climb up Catbells from the Keswick Launch, but most aim to take families off the beaten path to lesser known gems like Hampsfell, Hodbarrow,

At the main scramble on the Corridor Route, Scafell Pike (Adventure 20)

Stickle Pike or Sale Fell, or into wilder terrain like upper Ennerdale, the tops of Grange Fell and the remote mountain hostel at Skiddaw House.

Much has been written about the pressures of modern family life in a fast-paced screen-based world and there have even been reports of children suffering from 'nature deficit disorder' and forgetting how to play. The health and wellbeing benefits of having outdoor adventures as a family are clear. This book aims to help you fill your lungs with fresh air and nearly always have fun for free. Although some of the routes seem short, they are all memorable days out. They are designed so that families can do as little or as much as they want; stop to take in the stunning surroundings, learn new skills and get a good sense of achievement from their climbs, rides, hikes and finds.

Bases and transport

On paper, the Lake District is not huge at 2,292km^2, but it can feel much bigger when trying to get from one side to the other. Broadly speaking, the national park is pretty much everything west of the M6 motorway from a few miles south of Kendal to just shy of Penrith in the north. The park stretches west to include the coastline between Silecroft and Ravenglass, north of which the industry (particularly nuclear power) and larger towns such as Workington and Whitehaven in the vicinity mean that the protected area finishes a few miles inland. There are two main north-to-south artery

roads through the Lake District. The A592 links Kendal, Windermere and Ambleside to Keswick. It is useful for accessing Grasmere, Windermere, Thirlmere and Patterdale but understandably gets phenomenally busy, particularly on its narrower sections during peak periods. The A590/A595 is the most southerly route into Lakeland, leaving the M6 below Kendal and going round the coast to Broughton-in-Furness, Gosforth and north to Whitehaven. This also has slow sections but generally less traffic and is particularly useful for accessing Wasdale, Eskdale, Dunnerdale, Ennerdale and Coniston. More easterly areas such as Haweswater and Swindale are best accessed from Shap on the A6 and more northerly areas like Bassenthwaite and Derwentwater can be reached most simply by the A66 from Penrith.

For usability, we have split the routes in this book into northern and southern sections, as it would be unusual to attempt to do activities in the furthest extremes of the national park from the same base. Of course, there is some crossover, and places such as Grasmere might be equally accessible from both southern and northern bases. On the whole, the southern and central lakes see more visitors due to their accessibility, whereas the more remote areas to the north and west such as Ennerdale and Loweswater are less busy. Driving into many areas involves negotiating narrow roads with passing places and steep winding passes.

The Windermere area is a convenient base for the southern lakes (Adventure 8)

Public transport

The Lake District is well served by public transport and with a little fore-thought, the majority of the routes in this book can be reached without using a car. Rachel often went on holidays with her grandma to Keswick as a child and has fond memories of getting the bus to explore Borrowdale and Grasmere. The West Coast Mainline connecting London and Glasgow runs up the eastern side of the Lakes, stopping at Oxenholme near Kendal, Penrith and Carlisle. Branch lines connect Windermere and Staveley, Grange-over-Sands, and the west coast at Ravenglass and Whitehaven.

Stagecoach operates an extensive bus network in the national park, connecting all the bigger villages. A route map can be downloaded from www. stagecoachbus.com or a more useful comprehensive timetable is widely available at rail stations and tourist information centres. The biggest hubs for the bus network are Keswick and Windermere. There are between 5 and 10 buses per day on the more popular routes. See individual route information boxes for more public transport details.

Bases

The Lake District is Britain's most popular national park so it stands to reason that the main centres can get crowded, particularly in school holidays.

In the south, Bowness, Windermere and Ambleside, along with Grasmere and Coniston to a lesser extent, are the main villages that have amenities and plentiful accommodation. Campers are better placed to get away from the hustle and bustle; sites that are near the main centres without being too close can be a good compromise. The south-western corner of the park is by far the quietest part of the area to base yourself, but it is not as convenient for adventures around the central lakes of Windermere, Coniston Water and Grasmere.

In the north, Keswick is by far the most popular base. With excellent amenities, it is always lively but never seems quite as crowded as the honey-pots of the southern lakes. There are plenty of good campsites in its vicinity. Other good bases are the Ullswater pair of Pooley Bridge and Patterdale in the east. You wouldn't go too far wrong basing yourself near the attractive market town of Cockermouth, which is less than two miles outside the national park boundary on its north-western fringe.

When to go
This book is designed with the logic that most families will be visiting between April–October, particularly during the Easter, May, summer and October standard school holidays. That is not to say that many of the routes cannot be enjoyed in the winter months (Lakeland undoubtedly looks especially beautiful under a blanket of snow), but adults should be aware that venturing into a winter mountain environment with children requires far more planning and awareness of the potential serious risks involved. The harder hikes in this book can often be in winter climbing condition as late as April, requiring crampons, ice axes and mountaineering expertise. Trips on the water are best left until the summer months, but biking and lower altitude adventures could work well on a bright winter's day.

The Lake District is renowned for its changeable weather. Families would be lucky to spend a completely dry week there at any time of year. August is traditionally the wettest summer month – particularly irritating when it coincides with the long summer school holidays. May and June are generally more settled. Thankfully, rain is no obstacle to having fun on many of the routes but it is much safer to wait for clear weather for the fell top routes, which can be dangerous in poor visibility.

Hiking with children
Young children can move remarkably fast when they want to but, in our experience, a walk with young children doubles or triples the amount of time it would take mum or dad going solo. Older children hike quickly but still like to stop and mess about and eat mountains of food. This book aims to embrace all of the above and the routes are designed to be undertaken with a relaxed approach that includes plenty of pauses for fun.

Every family is different so it is futile to give too much general advice, but here are a few things that have helped us keep our sanity when hiking as a family:
- Going at the pace of the slowest member or stopping to wait at regular intervals can help stop young children becoming demoralised.

Fun and adventure whatever the season
(clockwise from top left: Adventure 28;
Adventure 17; Adventure 16; Adventure 33)

On the Swindale approach to Mosedale Cottage (Adventure 5)

- Building children's experience slowly by gradually increasing mileage, ascent and difficulty of terrain gives them achievable objectives.
- Encouraging a positive mindset and praising effort works well alongside knowing when your children have reached their limits and always being prepared to curtail plans or turn around.
- Giving children time to just embrace being outdoors in a beautiful place and stopping to play can recharge the batteries, as can having a good selection of enticing food to eat along the way.

All the routes that involve hiking are designed with an objective in mind, whether it is a fell top, cave, waterfall or even a picnic spot. These destinations can be a helpful focus for some children, as can the incentive of a treat when they get there. Parents will know that younger children often need distracting from the idea that they are doing a walk. Children build up hiking stamina quickly and many kids at the upper end of the range covered in this book may be much stronger hikers than their parents. Even younger children can be amazingly adept hikers, given time, practice and encouragement – some may even relish the idea of carrying a rucksack.

Equipment

This book is not aimed at parents of very young children who prefer to go on buggy walks (although we have made clear where this would be a possibility). Front and back carriers are the key to unlocking outdoors adventures with very young children. Babies and small children up to the age of three are

Babies can be remarkably portable – getting out of the carrier to enjoy the view from the top of the Old Man (Adventure 17)

remarkably portable. A **front carrier** for very young babies and, from around six months (or when baby's neck strength is sufficient) a good-quality **back carrier** with a rain cover and sun shade are invaluable pieces of kit that can unlock the outdoors. Back carriers in particular enable your child to experience more exciting outdoor environments with the family from an early age; he or she has a great view, often falls asleep en route and mum or dad gets fit carrying the extra weight! Best of all, toddlers can be encouraged to walk some of the way and then have a nap on a parent's back.

It is worth investing in decent equipment for children – wet feet and soggy bodies can make for miserable kids. Wearing hiking boots and taking waterproofs is best for all walks and essential on higher and more remote mountain terrain. Children are notoriously fickle about their body temperatures and seem to go from 'freezing' to 'boiling' within seconds. It can be frustrating and bulky packing fleeces, waterproofs, gloves and hats and getting them in and out of the rucksack on an out-of-season hike but this equipment is key to having a positive and safe experience.

Parents should be confident at map reading. Do not rely on mobile devices for route finding as signal can be poor and battery life limited.

Biking with children

There's no getting away from the fact that cycling with children can be a faff; getting the equipment ready, transporting it and finding suitable routes can be tricky. But the rewards of going cycling as a family are terrific and there are plenty of places in the Lake District to hire bikes and biking equipment if you don't want to bring your own. (A list of the most useful for routes in this book is in Appendix B). Many children love riding their bikes and can go faster and further than on foot, it is great exercise and learning to cycle is a key skill. The Lake District's road network is under huge pressure (particularly in school holidays with the volume of cars on the narrow winding roads) so we have gone to great lengths to avoid it. In this book all the cycling routes are essentially traffic-free. Some longer options by necessity have short sections on road, which are clearly marked and manageable for most families with care. The routes chosen aim to allow young cyclists to develop their skills safely and reach wilder places.

Equipment

Young children can be superbly transportable by bike. From when a baby can sit up unsupported for prolonged periods at around nine months to about four years old, rear-mounted **bike seats** are an affordable and popular option – all but the Whinlatter route in this book are possible using these. **Bike trailers** are less easy to pack but some argue they are less off-balancing for the adult cyclist. **Tag-alongs** and **towbars** where your child's bike is connected to yours are increasingly popular and allow children who are not yet confident or strong cyclists to ride their own bike. It is unlikely you will invest in all of these unless you are a regular cyclist, but there is always a way to make a bike ride work for your family.

A child seat is great until your child can manage a flat mile or two on a balance bike, first pedal bike or with stabilisers. At this stage many parents find it easier to walk or run alongside. If there are two adults, an older sibling might extend the route with one parent. By

Tag-along towbar bike set-up at Wray Castle (Adventure 8)

the age of five or six, many children are ready for their first geared bike and this opens up a wealth of extra possibilities. We have made clear by the grading system which routes are best left until children can ride up short hills. Older or more confident children will love the technical challenges provided by the Quercus trail and longer Great Langdale route. As with hiking, some older children may well become more confident cyclists than mum or dad!

Children, including those on bike seats, should always have a well-fitting helmet. Lights are a good idea and children love bike bells, which are very useful on multi-use paths like the Keswick Railway Ride. The current advice for cycling on roads still makes sense for traffic-free rides: cycle behind the children or with an adult at the front and back.

Getting wet

It wouldn't be a family holiday in the Lake District without getting on or into the water at some point and there are great adventures to be had with or without getting wet. Parents should adopt a particularly cautious approach to water-based activities, build up experience slowly and pay meticulously close attention to children.

In the water

The dramatically situated lakes are what makes the area so unique and its mountain streams, tarns and pools will equally delight children. Paddling and skimming stones on pebbly beaches are a must for children of all ages and we have highlighted in the text where this is possible on routes that are predominantly cycle rides or focussed on other activities. Depending on the

Riding away from the Langdale Pikes on the Great Langdale Trail (Adventure 2)

weather, there are several routes where some children may want to get wetter still and go swimming. Wild swimming by the shores of lakes and rivers, while looking up at the sky and the mountains, is a real sensory pleasure. It will bring squeals of wild excitement, but it does come with a few cautionary notes. Children should be particularly closely supervised near or in the water and even children who are confident swimmers should not be allowed to swim unaccompanied. Do not let children enter the water before an adult has checked the depth, temperature and current. Young swimmers should be supervised in the water on a one adult to one child basis. Make sure that the adult accompanying the child is a competent swimmer. Do not assume that children who can swim in a heated indoor pool will be able to do so in fresh water. Children get cold quickly. Basic short wetsuits can enable them to get the most out of going in the water. Wearing water shoes or tough sandals also makes it easier to get in and out at rocky shores.

Any paddling or swimming spots mentioned in this guide have only been thoroughly checked by the authors in warm, low water conditions. Innocuous-seeming mountain streams can become dangerous raging torrents after prolonged heavy rain. Always use your judgement, checking the depth, current and temperature and erring on the side of caution. Although the Lake District National Park includes quite a significant stretch of seashore – from Ravenglass down to Silecroft – the Lakeland coast is much maligned. This is at least partly justified due to the endless mudflats and proximity of the

Kayakers near Glencoyne Bay on Ullswater (Adventure 26)

Sellafield nuclear reprocessing plant to the north. Nonetheless, we have included three adventures in this book with options to visit coastal beaches, each of which is far away from the Sellafield area, just outside the national park to the south and north (adventures 11, 35 and 38). Always wash hands before eating if you have been in the water or on the beach.

On the water

The Lake District is one of the best places in Britain to get onto the water in a boat, with easy access and an enticing array of coves, bays and islands to explore. Being out on the water provides mesmerising views and experiences that you won't get anywhere else, while learning to handle a boat is great fun for children. In all of the 'on the water' routes, we have included the most up-to-date details of where to hire a vessel – mainly rowing boats, kayaks and canoes (refer to Appendix C). Increasingly, families for whom the boating bug has bitten are using their own equipment. Two, three or even four-seater inflatable kayaks, which can be packed into a standard car roof box, are the most popular and affordable choice. These range from glorified rubber dinghies to sturdy and rugged adventure equipment. Do your research and look for quality: some of the inflatable boats on the market are alarmingly cheap, unstable, flimsy and hard to steer.

You will need life jackets for all members of the family who are not strong swimmers and buoyancy aids for those who are.

Check your equipment for signs of damage before every outing and clean equipment after use to prevent the spread of invasive species.

None of the islands visited on routes in this book are more than a few hundred metres from shore but common sense still needs to prevail. Don't go out in windy conditions and know your capabilities. Children should sit in front or in the middle of adults in the boat. A dry bag for your phone, first aid kit, cash and picnic is recommended.

Wild nights: camping, bothying and hostelling

Whether it is snuggling up beneath the stars in a cosy sleeping bag or trekking high up a mountainside to stay in a youth hostel only accessible on foot, there is plenty of scope for overnight outdoor adventures in the Lake District. A carefully planned wild night is a superbly satisfying experience and your children can be real backpackers, carrying all they need.

Camping

With scores of official sites in fantastic locations, camping has perennially been a popular and relatively inexpensive choice for families in the Lake District. Despite the increase in glamping and the proliferation of yurts, pods, log cabins and the like, there are fortunately still many traditional small campsites on farms and by lakes with streams running through them. There are too many to list in this guide but details of almost all are widely available on the websites mentioned in Appendix E.

Wild camping

At the moment wild camping is unofficially tolerated in the Lake District if certain guidelines are followed (see

'Hold on tight, dad!' rope swing near Stonethwaite campsite (Adventure 28)

below). A responsible and respectful approach is key to ensuring that this tolerance continues and wild camping is a great way to teach your kids about human impact on the environment. While camping to most families means roomy tents, inflatable mattresses, pillows and camping chairs, wild camping with the family is utterly dependant on your ability to pack light. It is certainly a challenge, but the pay-off is your very own mountain berth in a perfect spot with no sound except the occasional bird, sheep or mountain stream, under huge starry skies with 360-degree views. Your children will remember it forever.

The wild camping guidelines are:

- Camp on open land above the highest fell wall far away from farms, villages and roads. Leave the area pristine. However tempting it might seem, do not light fires.
- Take away all litter (don't bury it). For good karma collect any litter other people have left behind. Do not leave food waste of any type to decompose.
- Go to the toilet at least 50m from water. Bury poo and carry toilet paper back out with you. Human poo bags (some containing special absorbent gel) are becoming de rigeur and even mandatory in other countries where the natural environment is becoming polluted by wild campers. These are available online.
- Camp as unobtrusively as possible: in small groups of one or two small tents, staying only one night, arriving late and leaving early. Ideally, use green tents to blend in if possible.

Family wild camping works best when the children carry at least their own sleeping bags and mats and children are old enough to be able to walk unaided to the camp location. Use a small tent and take the minimum amount of clothes for the trip. Boil water from a stream, rather than carrying all you'll need. Hand sanitiser gel can be useful after wild toilet trips. Try to steer clear of 'popular' and more intrusive spots for wild camping by major footpaths and at well-known tarns. Ennerdale permits camping in some areas of the valley above the fell wall.

Camping wild near Dunnerdale

Composing a careful entry in the bothy visitors' book (Adventure 5)

Bothying

The bothies mentioned in this book are mountain shelters located in wild and adventurous places. They are open to all and managed by the Mountain Bothies Association (mountainbothies. org.uk). There is no charge to stay, but users are expected to abide by the code below.

At first glance this might sound too good to be true but families should bear in mind that these are very rudimentary shelters. There is no booking system and you must be prepared to share the space with others. There are usually no toilet facilities and water usually comes from nearby springs or streams. If you or your children are fond of creature comforts then bothies are probably not for you. If in doubt, hike in to explore one of the bothies and see if you could imagine spending the night there.

THE BOTHY CODE

- Respect other users.
- Respect the bothy – take away all litter, report accidental damage, leave doors shut and tidy up.
- Respect the surroundings – use the bothy spade to bury poo over 200m from the bothy and water sources. Wash up downstream of the bothy. Bring your own fuel. Don't scavenge live wood or old fences to burn.
- Respect any seasonal restrictions of the landowner.
- Respect a restriction on groups of no more than six using bothies.

Youth hostels

There are many YHA hostels in great locations across the Lake District and staying can be a memorable adventure in itself. In popular spots the hostels are not the very low cost option that they once were – they now compete in a world of glamping and free Wi-Fi and the like. It is also worth bearing in mind that families with under-12s are now obliged to book a whole private family room rather than staying in dorms due to safeguarding concerns (and possibly the fear that children might disturb other users) – a subtle change of ethos which seems a shame. Information about all the youth hostels in the area is available at www.yha.org.uk.

Out of season it is possible to hire a whole youth hostel in many locations – a good option if you are planning a trip with other families.

Adventuring safely

Parents constantly perform a balancing act between wanting to keep their children safe and wanting to foster a sense of adventure in them. It can sometimes be a hard line to tread – children naturally want to push their limits and are not always tuned in to 'obvious' hazards such as steep edges and drops. We have tried to highlight points at which extra care should be taken, but wild outdoor environments can never be completely safe and we would not want them to be. Most parents accept the risks of nettle stings, grazed knees and ant bites as part of a natural learning process; not so broken

A gig with a view at Black Sail hostel in Ennerdale (Adventure 19)

bones, hypothermia or dehydration. Ultimately the adults in the party have full responsibility for the safety of the children. We make the assumption in this guide that adults using it will have some grounding and experience in outdoor environments: that they can read a map and know what to pack in their rucksack. Even so, adults should always err on the side of caution, particularly if conditions or the capabilities of any member of the party are in doubt. Adults should never expect children to do any activity that they would not be happy to do themselves.

It may sound unfashionably authoritarian, but the most important factor in having a successful and safe outdoor adventure is that the children understand that the adults are in charge and that if adults ask them to stop they must do so immediately. This is particularly important with children who love to run on ahead or go off 'hiding' or 'exploring'. The ultimate aim is to educate children so that gradually they can be given more responsibility and become aware of how to take care of themselves. It is also worth mentioning adventuring with other people's children: never assume that they have been given the same boundaries and teach your children not to blindly follow their peers. If you have been put in charge of other people's children, do not shy away from giving them firm instructions and rules before setting off.

For safety equipment associated with boating, see the On the water section. For all activities pack sun cream, warm clothing and waterproofs as appropriate along with adequate water and food. Always take a basic first aid kit on any outdoor adventure with children.

Ticks can be a particular hazard in outdoor environments. Children and adults should check their skin when washing. If anyone is bitten, remove the whole tick with sharp/pointed tweezers by gripping as close to the head as possible and using a steady straight pull without twisting, then apply antiseptic. Alternatively, specialised tick-removing devices are inexpensive and easily fit into first aid kits. These devices are stocked by most of the major outdoor retailers and are readily available online. Animals such as sheep and geese tend to poo in the great outdoors. Teach children to wash their hands properly after adventuring and, where this is not possible, consider using sanitiser gel to prevent upset tummies.

Responsible use of our national park

Over the 40 years that we have been coming on family holidays to the northern Lake District there have been huge changes. Increasing visitor numbers have put pressure on the infrastructure of the national park; the growing popularity of outdoor pursuits and a smorgasbord of both accurate and not-so-accurate information available online have been contributing factors.

In recent years the number of occasions we've seen burnt patches of grass or even discarded disposable barbecues by the lakeshores has become

Slate shards near the summit of Castle Crag (Adventure 32)

RESPECT OTHER PEOPLE

- Consider the local community and other people enjoying the outdoors.
- Leave gates and property as you find them and follow paths unless wider access is available.

Protect the natural environment:

- Leave no trace of your visit and take your litter home.
- Keep dogs under effective control.

Enjoy the outdoors:

- Plan ahead and be prepared.
- Follow advice and local signs.

alarmingly frequent. These might be extreme examples, but there also seem to be plenty of well-meaning parents who unwittingly add to the problems by letting their children climb dry stone walls, swing on gates and damage fences. Inconsiderate parking on narrow bus routes also increasingly raises tensions.

Without being 'the fun police', it is important to teach children how to follow the countryside code and help them have an understanding of the fragility of exceptional natural environments. It is a cliché, but the Lake District National Park will be in their hands in the future.

Getting close to nature

One of the real joys of outdoor adventuring with children is watching them interact with and play in nature, showing genuine wonder at its shapes, colours and textures. On routes in this book children can see red squirrels scurrying up trees, train their binoculars on massive ospreys guarding their nests in Dodd Wood, search for frogspawn and minnows or spot goldeneyes, grebes and geese on the lakes. They can catch crabs and scour rock pools at coastal Maryport or keep a low profile in the hide at Hodbarrow lagoon to spy oystercatchers and terns. Families can even search the skies above Haweswater to find the national park's one resident golden eagle, watch ravens circle the high fell tops and look out for peregrine falcons nesting in the crags. You may also be lucky enough to spot owls, red deer, otters and rare butterflies. For nature-lovers, the Lake District is full of excitement.

Most children will happily entertain themselves on a pebbly beach, a bouldery fellside or in a shadowy forest and outdoor imaginative play has been shown to be great for children's minds and bodies. Climbing trees is one activity for which lots of children show a natural inclination or aptitude and we have tried to highlight where a particularly excellent tree can be climbed on route. Many children also show an unwavering affection for commonplace natural 'toys' like sticks and stones. Finding and carrying a suitable walking stick can often give reluctant hikers a new lease of life and pooh sticks is a sure-fire winning game. Older children can be also taught to use a penknife or even a potato peeler safely for whittling – if you're not sure about how to do this, there is a downloadable guide at www.woodlandtrust.org.uk. Skimming stones is also a great skill to master.

Foraging for a wild snack on route can be immensely satisfying. Bilberries have always been a firm favourite in our family. In August the distinctive small purple berries seem

Nature's bounty –
bilberry gathering
on route to Skiddaw
House (Adventure 40)

Searching for sea creatures on Maryport beach (Adventure 38)

to grow everywhere on Lakeland fells, but we have harvested particularly bountiful crops on Sale Fell, Back o' Skiddaw, Loughrigg and Helm Crag. Slightly later in the season, blackberries are easy to find and wild strawberries or raspberries are a special treat if you can spot them. Whinlatter, Dodd and Grizedale forests are great for spotting mushrooms, but fungi foraging is high risk – best left to the experts or you could book a guided mushroom walk (see Appendix D).

Crabbing from the quay in Maryport is included in this guide – crabs do not seem overly worried by being caught and tipped back in by excited children. Trawling the shallows or rock pools with a bucket to find tiny creatures is a great waterside activity. Serious fishing is not included in the guide but it will come as no surprise

that the Lake District is a popular fishing area and patient children can find it surprisingly enjoyable. In England, adults need to have a fishing licence to catch freshwater fish such as salmon or trout. These are inexpensive and available from post offices. Three of the main lakes – Windermere, Ullswater and Coniston – are open to public fishing if you have your own tackle. Rookin House at Ullswater and Hawkshead Trout at Esthwaite Water offer organised fishing trips (refer to Appendix D for details).

How to use this guide and grading

The routes in this guide are split into northern and southern sections. The symbols in the contents pages provide a quick overview of the activities involved in each adventure, though many are optional.

The route information boxes at the start of each chapter are designed to give families an idea as to whether this adventure is for them. The routes are fairly inclusive and we have tried to provide options for both ambitious older children and those with toddlers in backpacks or on bike seats where possible. The 'suitable for' heading gives further information about whether a route is feasible for your family but we have shied away from guessing the ages at which children might manage certain activities. As a rule of thumb for this guide, 'younger children' refers to 3 to 6-year-olds and 'older children' to 7–12s. Children's hiking, biking and scrambling abilities vary immensely: some five and six-year-olds may not yet be able to ride a bike whereas others may happily zoom along for 20km or hike up Scafell Pike. Similarly, children's speed varies immensely. Where adults may walk at 3/4km an hour (or cycle off road at 16km an hour) children may take up to three times as long depending on their age and ability. A parent will have a good idea of their child's speed, but always factor in extra time. This guide intends to give you information to make route choices that you know are suitable for your children's abilities.

The Considerations section adds key information that adults may want to give some thought to before setting off. The parking areas at start points are given with a grid reference and the nearest village or area. Many of the convenient car parks are operated by the National Trust and members can park for free in them. Public transport options are also included where feasible. The Amenities heading gives details of places to buy refreshments and public toilets on route. If this heading is missing, bring a picnic.

Each adventure begins with an overview of what's involved, followed by a route description supported by Ordnance Survey mapping. Descriptions include harder and easier options if they are available. Route descriptions vary in length; some are more detailed, for example on high remote hiking terrain. Others, such as kayaking trips, provide a brief route outline with the aim of allowing parents to tailor the adventure to their own family. Advice about whether the routes are feasible in inclement weather and alternative rainy day plans are given.

Grading

We have colour graded the routes in ascending order of difficulty starting with green, followed by blue, red and then black. Of course this is a completely subjective assessment and green in this case means enjoyable for everyone given ample time rather than easy. There are dangers such as drops and edges on routes of all colours.

Hiking

In general, **green hikes** are on level terrain and good paths. They will be simple for older children in the 7 to 12-year-old category and manageable for younger children who can walk a few miles (3 to 6-year-olds). Green routes are particularly suitable for those who have outgrown a backpack but could be carried a little way on mum or dad's back should energy levels falter. We make the assumption that babies will be in carriers and toddlers may go in backpacks and walk some of the way. **Blue hikes** are still mainly on good paths with perhaps some easy scrambling sections or rockier terrain, more significant height gain or visits to lower summits. These routes are good achievements for the 7–12s and more of a challenge for the 3–6s. **Red routes** may challenge parents' map-reading skills, have a more serious remote element and longer stretches of tricky and vertiginous terrain. Some experienced five and six-year-olds may be able to tackle them and 7–12s will find them a good challenge. **Black routes** are long days out in big mountains – serious undertakings for both parents and children – and possibly involve harder scrambling. Build up experience slowly before tackling these.

Bike rides

All but the black-graded Quercus Trail are viable for adults with child seats and good bike-handling skills. All rides are possible on adult hybrid bikes and standard children's bikes. **Green routes** are there-and-back routes where very young riders from 3–6 years old who are unsteady (or are on balance bikes, stabilisers or scooters) can stretch their legs and do as much as is sensible. They are enjoyable for the whole family and simple for 7–12s and confident cyclists. **Blue routes** involve more ascent and may be round trips on less well made surfaces. They are challenging for under 7s and good achievements for 7–12s. **Red routes** involve greater distances on more difficult terrain. Children need bikes with gears and there may be sections where cyclists need to get off and push. Some experienced five and six-year-olds may manage these but most 7–12s will find them challenging. **Black routes** demand very good bike-handling skills and are technical challenges both for older children and adults.

Water-based activities

These are graded based on distance from shore; distance covered on water for the rowers or paddlers; and difficulty of landing, launching and navigating. All water activity grades also take account of summer-time low water depth, current and ease of access to the water. The on-the-water adventures make the assumption that adults will be handling the boat and that families will start off with a green or blue route and build up experience slowly.

The Southern Lakes

Adventure 1
Swallows and Amazons Island, Coniston

Boating to the island that inspired the famous children's adventure story, exploring and swimming

Start/finish	Coniston area. Roadside parking along the eastern shore of Coniston Water between (SD 295 914) and (SD 300 928) or Brown Howe car park (fee) on the western shore of the lake at (SD 290 910).
Distance	300m to 800m from the shore depending on launching spot
Suitable for	🟢 Green. In calm weather it is feasible for most well-equipped families with enough adult paddlers. Landing with young children is easy at the island's harbour.
Amenities	Public toilets at Brown Howe parking
Considerations	Refer to the On the water section in the introduction. The island does have cliffs and drops, so children must be closely supervised, particularly around the island's perimeter. Camping, barbecues and fires are not permissible on the island.
Caution	You are bound to spot at least one person doing the popular 3m water jump from the craggy spur on the south of the island – the jump is hazardous, it has rocks directly beneath it that are harder to clear than might be expected.

'Better drowned than duffers, if not duffers, won't drown'
– *Arthur Ransome, 1932*

Peel Island on Lake Coniston was the primary inspiration for Arthur Ransome's Wild Cat Island in the classic children's novel *Swallows and Amazons*. Today it belongs to us all through the stewardship of the National Trust. It can be a very popular kayaking and canoeing destination on summer weekends – but this is part of its appeal as children running wild among its various nooks and crannies pretending to be Nancy Blackett-style pirates and other such terrors of the seas bring it to life. This is also a good place for children to befriend other 'scurvy dogs' to play with. A perfect sheltered 'hidden harbour' allows for the easy mooring of boats and is

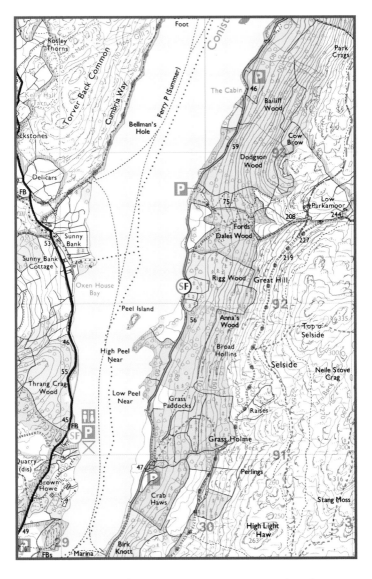

shallow enough to disembark youngsters without trouble. The island has ample room and there is just the right amount to explore – although do not expect peace and tranquillity among the calls of 'sea snake' and 'blackguard' from scoundrels threatening to make you walk the plank!

Simply paddle to the island. The 'hidden harbour' is on the southwest side of the island and can be reached steadily enough from either the east or west side. The harbour is ideal and should not be difficult to locate. There are trees to climb, slabs to scramble up, channels to swim and paths to be explored – enjoy.

Bad weather alternative
Not suitable for bad weather. Visit Tarn Hows or Wray Castle instead.

Note: Kayaks, canoes and rowing boats can be hired at Coniston Boating Centre – SD 307 970. Unfortunately, Peel Island is more than 5km to the south of the centre and, unless you are of a very high paddling or rowing standard, it is far too far to realistically reach from the centre, explore the island and still have energy for the return – it might be an impossible excursion if there is any wind about. Those hiring boats can still have an adventure exploring the bays to the south of Coniston village.

A greeting party at the secret harbour on Wild Cat Island

Adventure 1 – Swallows and Amazons Island, Coniston

Spying other pirates on Wild Cat Island

Adventure 2

Great Langdale Bike Trail, Elterwater and Skelwith Force

Two traffic-free cycling options with a visit to a waterfall

Start/finish	Short route: Elterwater, National Trust car park (SD 327 047). Long route: Great Langdale, the smaller and most easterly of the two Stickle Ghyll National Trust car parks (SD 296 064).
Distance	5km (3.1 miles) there and back; 15km (9.3 miles) there and back for the longer route.
Suitable for	●● Green or red. The shorter route is green for all ages and is just level enough for bikes with stabilisers. It's possible and enjoyable as a walk and with an all-terrain buggy. The longer route is red – practically traffic-free but only suitable for older children who are proficient cyclists as it has some climbing, steep descents and stony surfaces.
Amenities	Cafés at Skelwith Bridge, Elterwater, Great Langdale and Chapel Stile. Public toilets at Elterwater, Great Langdale Stickle Ghyll car park.
Considerations	Many walkers use this route – warn children how to pass them safely. A short section on both routes passes a steep drop to the river. Children should be kept away from the edge when cycling. The longer route has sections on both farm and quarry tracks where cyclists might well come across vehicles. The scrambly rocks at the foot of Skelwith Force are very slippery when damp.

This trip alongside Great Langdale Beck and past Elter Water to the impressive Skelwith Force ticks plenty of the boxes for a great family day out. It has a standard option for younger families and an excellent tougher extension for those wanting to burn off excess energy on the Great Langdale Trail. The Langdale Pikes, which rear their distinctive heads above the glacial valley, and the watery spectacles of Skelwith Force and Elter Water provide some wonderful scenery as you ride. There is very little ascent and descent on the easier route, which is traffic-free and waymarked. The longer route is hillier (most children will wheel their bike up one or two climbs). Paddling spots can be found along the beck on both routes.

Short route

The riverside cycle and walking path starts from the bottom of the car park and heads SE. There are a few cobbled and bumpy sections here but it doesn't get any rougher. Follow the river to a bend where the path enters **Rob Rash Wood**. Look out to your right for a climbing tree on the bend here. As you exit the wood, Elter Water comes into view.

> Elter Water, meaning 'lake of the swans', has a small pebbly beach and swans can often be spotted here.

Continue across lovely pastures where sheep graze until a small rise brings you to a bridge above **Skelwith Force**. Leave bikes here and scramble carefully down to feel the force of the waterfall.

Do not cross the bridge but continue on the same bank of the river to eventually emerge at some houses and the back of Chester's café. Take on board some well-earned cake or ice-cream and then retrace your outbound journey to the start point.

Extended route

Follow blue cycling signs for Ambleside out of the Stickle Ghyll car park and down a wide track with splendid views of the Langdale Pikes behind you. After 1.6km, where the track turns left to join the valley road, take a bridleway rightwards through gates. It will then fork right again and lead to a gated bridge across **Great Langdale Beck**.

Go through **Oak Howe Farm** and continue straight ahead on the bridleway towards Chapel Stile and Ambleside. The route first climbs steeply and then more gradually through woods for 1.2km to reach **Baysbrown Farm**. Continue straight on through this, joining the surfaced farm road for 1km. Look out for a cycling sign left to **Chapel Stile**. Initially, this is a fairly steep gravelly descent so take particular care.

Perfect family cycling on the flat track from Elterwater

Getting ready for the big climb after crossing Great Langdale Beck

The bridleway leads down through a working quarry (watch out for quarry vehicles particularly on week days) to the Chapel Stile Bridge. Do not cross this into the village, but continue right along the riverside to eventually join the quarry access track (possibility of large access vehicles) and emerge at **Elterwater** where the short route is joined by going left over the road bridge to the car park. Retrace your outbound route on the way back.

Bad weather alternative
The shorter trip is feasible in most weather conditions.

An old road sign points along the track near Chapel Stile

Great Langdale
Dungeon Ghyll 2¾

Adventure 3
Tarn Hows geocaching

Finding hidden treasure on a circuit of the lake

Start/finish	Coniston area. National Trust parking at (SD 326 994). Tarn Hows is signed from the B5285 Coniston to Hawkshead road.
Distance	3km (1.9 miles) or 5km (3.1 miles) for longer route
Suitable for	●● Green or longer blue route. Very little height gain and mainly on easy paths. The shorter route could be done with a pushchair, keeping to the main path and not finding the geocaches.
Amenities	An ice cream van is often in the car park. There are toilets there too.
Public transport	Bus 505 from Windermere to High Cross 2km away.

Tarn Hows feels like the Lake District in miniature with its tiny lake and fells. As if the numerous balancing logs, climbing trees and paddling beaches were not enough to entice families, Tarn Hows proves the ideal first geocaching experience, a local school having set up a trail of 10 small hidden plastic boxes of 'treasure' to locate on route (see geocaching box below). Seven caches are accessible from subsidiary paths off the main shorter trail, whereas a further two are slightly outlying on the extended route. The caches make use of natural features and the 'clues' on the App lead seekers to see hidden corners of Tarn Hows such as a 'cannon' and a 'snowflake' formed by trees. The popular walk around the water's edge only clocks up a diminutive 2.5km – miniscule enough to be manageable for even very young walkers. Adding the optional extra dimension of a geocaching treasure hunt makes the shortest route a round 3km and the longer option 5km. There are numerous paddling and picnicking spots on route.

From the car park, take the path around the western side of the lake (left when looking out from the car park). Continue on this well-made path with deviations onto more minor trails to find the caches. The second of the caches is located up a path beside a stream where there is a child-friendly fallen tree bridge. All the caches are near to vague paths but only the main path is buggy friendly. For the extended route,

Tarn Hows – one of Beatrix Potter's favourite walks

Geocaching

For parents new to geocaching, rest assured that all you need is a smartphone with the free www. geocaching.com App. The App is fairly self-explanatory and many technologically minded children will catch on extremely quickly in order to find the hidden caches. It is worth bearing in mind that, should your children wish to take any 'treasures'

Treasure hunter finding a cache

from the caches, they should leave something of equal or higher value in its place: take a few stickers, marbles or badges for this purpose. Detractors might well say that geocaching amounts to glorified littering, but with hundreds of thousands of caches now in situ in the UK, it is something that is here to stay. On the positive side, geocaching genuinely seems to inspire some children who might otherwise prefer to be inside to interact with the outdoors environment.

look out for a split off left signed to Skelwith near the far end of the tarn. Take this, turning right towards Hawkshead after 300m on a stony track. Return via a grassy path through a gate after 300m. Note that one cache is actually 250m further along the stony track at the turn to **Iron Keld**.

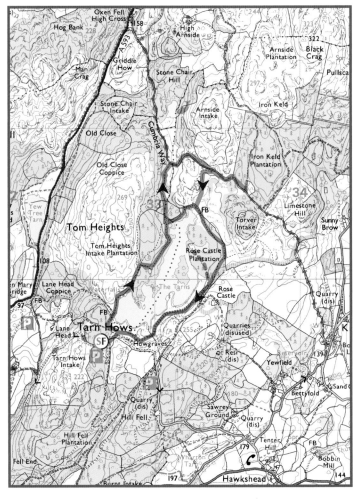

The grassy path descends to regain the head of the tarn and the main path is followed leftwards all the way back to the parking area with a short deviation on a path after 600m to the 'cannon' (a massive fallen tree to climb) and to find **Rose Castle** – a hidden cottage in the woods.

Bad weather alternative
The shorter walk should be feasible in most conditions.

Did you know?

- Beatrix Potter loved the Tarn Hows estate and bought it in 1930 in order to stop it being sold off in pieces for development. She later sold it at cost and partly donated it to the National Trust.

Nature's bridges: the Tarn Hows circuit

Adventure 4
Cathedral Caves

Exploring the cave tunnels of a former quarry, scrambling and paddling

Start/finish	Skelwith Bridge area. Parking area at Hodge Close (NY 318 019). From the A593, take a single track road at High Yewdale signed to Hodge Close only.
Distance	5km (3.1 miles)
Suitable for	● Blue. Very little height gain and mainly on easy paths. Manageable for most families.
Amenities	The Three Shires Inn in Little Langdale sells ice cream, food and drink.
Public transport	Nearest in Skelwith Bridge (bus 516 from Ambleside)
Considerations	Extra close supervision should be given to children, particularly near the edges in the upper tier of Cathedral Caves and if you venture anywhere near the terrifying drop into the massive Hodge Close Quarry near the start of the route. Bring head-torches and wellies or a change of footwear as a couple of the tunnels are often wet. Read the safety information about the caves before entering the site.

Children have Lakeland author Beatrix Potter to thank for the adventures they will have exploring Cathedral Caves. The caves, also known as Little Langdale Quarries, were bought by Potter in 1929 and subsequently gifted to the National Trust, which has kept them open to the public. Where adults might view the former slate quarry as a historical curiosity, children seem to delight in exploring its gloomy tunnels and find an echoey magic in the immense arched main chamber after which the caves are named. Besides the caves, this trip will fascinate some children with a glimpse (from nowhere near the edge) or even a detour down into the incredibly dramatic quarry workings at Hodge Close and its gargantuan slate spoil heaps. If all this sounds industrial and unappealing, be reassured that this is a fascinating and beautiful trip with views of the Langdale Fells. As well as superb walking, it provides an insight into the history of Lakeland industry and its impact on the landscape.

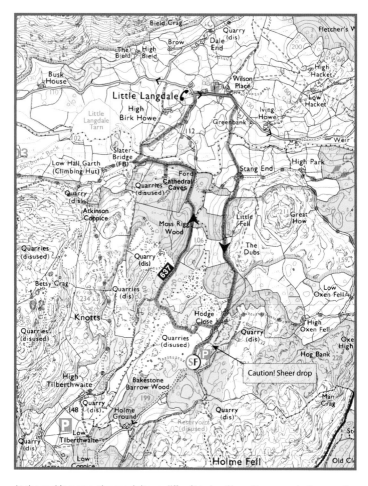

At the parking area, the precipitous cliffs of Hodge Close Quarry are just across the road behind a small fence. **The treacherous scree and boulder descent direct from the car park towards the murky quarry pool is absolutely not suitable for children. The only suitable way into the abyss is described at the end of the main route description.**

Getting spooked in Cathedral Cave

From the parking area, continue along the road for a short distance (a small path to a view of the stomach-churning drop into the quarry leaves rightwards after 50m). At a collection of buildings with a bungalow on the right, take the gated track left downhill. After another gateway, take the middle of three tracks descending through woodland to cross a beck. Turn right at another track, passing more **quarry tips** and eventually open fields to the right. Stay on this track for 1km until it meets a small road at a bend. Do not take the road, but descend left on the track towards a bridge and ford. Don't cross but turn left here. After 50m or so, look out for a stile in the wall to your left and a sign about the Atkinson Coppice and its caves. Take the stile and the path up the hillside, bearing right to reach the main cave entrance after about 100m. A short tunnel leads into the enormous main chamber. Another leads from it and via a short easy scramble up onto the second tier. Here, there are several tunnels to explore, but take care as there is a serious drop back down into the main **Cathedral Cave**. One tunnel leads to a lesser cavern and a couple lead nowhere, but the longer one at the bottom of the obvious main cliff (this has a guard rail at the start) eventually emerges at a higher platform above the entrance to the main cave. From here, a path leads down to rejoin our route or up to a third tier where there is yet another tunnel.

Having rejoined the route at the track beside the River Brathay, continue for about 300m then take a stile and gate leading rightwards to cross the river at the lovely **Slater Bridge**.

Slater Bridge is a 300-year-old tiny slate packhorse bridge. The river here is a great spot for picnicking, paddling and rock-hopping to the grassy island.

Shortly beyond the bridge, turn right through a gap in the wall and take the path gently uphill across open land. There are ample scrambling opportunities for children here on the small outcrops adorning the nearby hillside.

After 400m turn left on the single track road then right at the next junction into **Little Langdale**. Walk past the pub and after 100m turn right on a path signposted to **Stang End**. Cross a footbridge and go up to Stang End Farm, which has an old wool spinning gallery. Here, turn left then immediately right on a track signposted to Hodge Close. Stay on the track all the way to reach the road at **Hodge Close**.

Crossing Slater Bridge

The imposing cliffs of Hodge Close quarry

Continue through a gate and straight on to the car park or, if enthusiasm remains, you can visit the deep dark **Hodge Close Quarry** pool (slightly harder than the rest of the route) from a path leaving the road 50m beyond the aforementioned gate. Take the track left signed to High Oxen Fell. Follow this for 30m to a gap in a fence on the right where an initially scrambly path leads down through an overgrown quarry to emerge at a cavern by the spooky pool.

Bad weather alternative
A shorter walk to Cathedral Cave can be made directly from Little Langdale. There is very little parking available.

Did you know?

- The evil-looking Hodge Close Quarry has been the macabre scene of the deaths of several divers who have got lost in the labyrinthine tunnels and depths beneath its black pool.

- There is a 70m drop down from the quarry's edge and the pool is 20m deep.

- When photographed from certain angles, the reflection of the cliffs form an uncanny likeness of a skull, adding to the spooky ambience of the quarry.

- The Lakeland green slate mined at Cathedral Caves can still be seen adorning the roofs of many houses and in walls.

Adventure 5
Mosedale Cottage Backpacking

Visiting or staying the night at a remote mountain bothy

Start/finish	Longsleddale. Small parking area where the road ends at Sadgill (NY 483 057).
Distance	5.6km (3.5 miles) one way
Suitable for	● Red. Around 300m height gain on the way to the bothy and 50m on the return.
Considerations	Bothies provide very basic accommodation for which there is no charge. Read the bothy code beforehand and respect its rules for dealing with human waste and water sources (see notes in Introduction). Groups of more than six people should not use bothies and families should expect that there could be others using the bothy at the same time. Check www.mountainbothies.org.uk before setting off. Do not set off in poor visibility.

There is something unequivocally exciting about staying in a remote stone building miles away from any roads and without the usual comforts of electricity and running water. Even hiking up to pay a visit or make a hot drink at Mosedale Cottage feels adventurous and the quiet trip on a disused quarry track up lovely Longsleddale beside the River Sprint is a worthwhile excursion in itself. Mosedale is downright luxurious by the standards of most bothies, boasting sofas in a separate living room, but families should be prepared to have a rough and ready adventure in beautiful but spartan surroundings. The experience of backpacking in and carrying everything you need is feasible for the majority of families with careful planning. By showing children how to care for a unique communal space like Mosedale, we can help secure the survival of bothies.

Follow the track from the road's end gradually up beside the river. The track steepens for a short section after 2km as it passes the cliffs of Goat Scar and **Buckbarrow Crag** and the waterfalls of **Cleft Ghyll**. There are a few spots where the river can be accessed for picnicking and paddling. The track levels out again after a further 1km near the disused **Wrengill Quarry**.

Those with boundless energy can walk up a path to the left beyond the quarry ruins for 600m to reach a waterfall and cavern.

Beside the River Sprint near Cleft Ghyll on the Sadgill approach

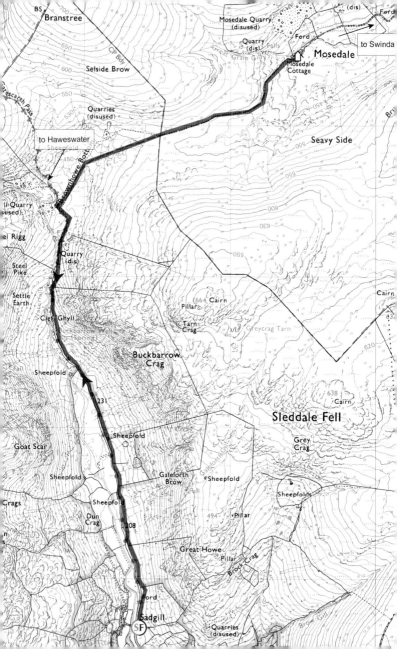

At the quarry, look out for a signpost to Swindale and Wetsleddale pointing to the right over the river. Take this grassy path winding up the hillside to a col and after another 1km, walk through a gate in a fence. The last 1.5km to the bothy can often be boggy and the path is less distinct. You will head roughly north-east and descend slightly to **Mosedale Cottage**, which soon becomes visible. Return by the same route.

Alternative routes

There are alternative approaches to Mosedale Cottage:

- From the larger parking area at Mardale Head at the southern end of Haweswater NY 469 107 (a similar distance but more ascent).

- From the small designated parking area 3.4km from the end of the single track Swindale road NY 521 141 (longer but passing the lovely cascades of Mosedale Beck near the head of Swindale).

- From the car park at Wet Sleddale reservoir NY 554 114 (boggier, as the name suggests).

Making friends with a frog at Mosedale Cottage

Adventure 6

The Lion and the Lamb – Helm Crag and Grasmere

Climbing a Lakeland landmark and scrambling on the summit ridge

Start/finish	Grasmere village. Free parking on the outskirts and several paid car parks.
Distance	5km (3.1 miles) with 350m ascent
Suitable for	● Blue – on a fairly steep and rocky path.
Amenities	Grasmere has public toilets and a good choice of refreshments including its famous gingerbread.
Considerations	There are some sections of walking on a minor dead-end road. There are sizeable crags with considerable drops near the route. Do not let children wander off when scrambling.

The Lion and the Lamb can be found lying in wait at the very top of the 396m Helm Crag, the iconic fell overlooking the honey-pot village and lake of Grasmere. From the valley floor, children can easily make out the profiles of the animal-shaped rocks on its summit ridge and then make the short but steep journey up the craggy hillside to scramble along the crest. Besides the two beasts, there are rocks resembling an old woman playing the organ and a Howitzer gun as well. The well-trodden path from Grasmere is always interesting, but the terrain is tricky enough to scupper the least confident young hikers so it is not recommended as a very first fell walk. The attractions of Grasmere village will prove an enticement at the end of the route – with its world-famous gingerbread shop being a perennial favourite.

Leave the village by a road on the bend near the village green and opposite the Little Inn, which is signed to Allen Bank. After 100m turn right towards **Goody Bridge**. There are some good boulders for warm-up scrambling here. This route joins a path parallel to **Easedale Road** for 300m then continues for 200m on the minor road. Ignore a sign straight on to Helm Crag and instead cross a stone footbridge over **Easedale Beck** to the left, where there is a good paddling and pooh sticks spot. After a further 200m, turn right over a humpbacked bridge to rejoin the termination of the road. Turn left then immediately right up a stone track with a large carving of an owl

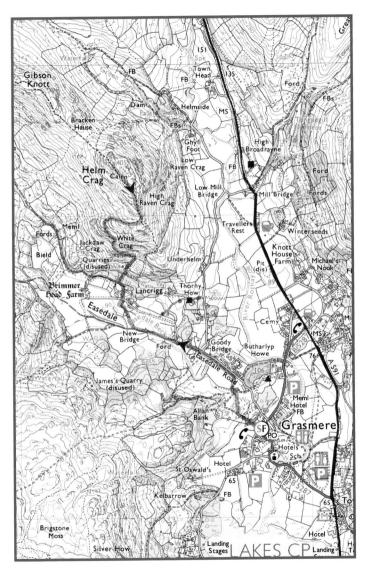

Climbing the keys of the old lady's organ at the Howitzer rocks on Helm Crag

at its head. After 50m, turn right following a sign to Helm Crag and start climbing on the main path zigzagging up to **Jackdaw Crag**, where there is a murky swamp beneath the crag itself and a suitable tree to climb. Continue trending left to reach a shoulder of bracken with views into Easedale and the lake of Grasmere. The path swings back rightwards to reach the summit ridge at a larger shoulder.

Head up the ridge with a little very easy scrambling. Here, the first large rocks will come into sight – the lion and lamb. On this approach, the lamb appears to have rather a long neck and the best impression of the two beasts is looking back from a little further along the ridge. It is great fun to scramble up the ridge here to end up on the lion's mane. Do not let youngsters go on ahead to the highest point of the lion's head as there is a terrifying drop between the lion and the lamb (the latter is no place for scrambling and a far more dangerous creature).

Continue along the ridge to the Howitzer set of rocks. There is good scrambling on the lower far end of the group but severe drops mean children need close supervision. The highest point of the crag at the Howitzer itself is only reached by a Grade 2 scramble. **It is not suitable for children.**

Return by the same route – do not be tempted by other paths leading off the summit. The authors have painstakingly explored these and they are to be avoided.

Bad weather alternative
On days where the soggy lion and lamb are hidden underneath thick rain clouds, Grasmere provides shelter in the Wordsworths' eerie home of Dove Cottage.

Helm Crag

Helm Crag is either guarded by the lion and lamb, or by a protruding Howitzer gun, depending on your point of view. From the Grasmere road at the Swan Hotel, the lion and lamb shapes for which the fell is named are clear. From the A591 at Dunmail Rise, the north-western end of the summit ridge is much more pronounced, with the obvious Howitzer gun pointing out from the fell top. The Howitzer rocks, when viewed from the ridge, can also be made to resemble a 'lion couchant' or lying down lion and the smaller rocks beyond, the 'lamb'. From the path beside them, the Howitzer group are also said to look like an old lady playing the organ. Confusing? Let your children decide which name fits best.

The lion and the lamb basking together in the evening sun

Did you know?

- Victorian cook Sarah Nelson developed her secret recipe for Grasmere gingerbread in 1854. This sweet and spicy cross between a biscuit and a cake is quite unique and a great treat for young fell-walkers.

Adventure 7
Rydal Caves and Loughrigg

Visiting caves, scrambling, climbing a fell, paddling in Rydal Water

Start/finish	Rydal. Brant Bows car park (NY 365 060). If full, there is additional parking in Rydal (from this, take the footpath opposite the pub over a footbridge to join the main route).
Distance	1km (0.6 miles) to caves; red option 7.5km (4.7 miles); green option 4.5km (2.8 miles); blue option 7km (4.3 miles). There is 270m ascent to Loughrigg summit.
Suitable for	● ● ● Red, green or blue. Options for all ages. All families can explore the upper cave and complete the lower level walk. The lower cave and summit climb are more challenging undertakings.
Amenities	Tea room in Rydal. Nearest public toilets at Grasmere.
Public transport	Bus 555 from Keswick or Windermere.
Considerations	A difficult 4m scramble is required to enter the lower cave – a one-adult-to-one-child ratio is advised. The harder route option is only advised in good visibility and requires parents to have decent navigational skills. Take head-torches.

The excitement of getting into Rydal Caves far outweighs the interest once inside. The main cave can usually only be gained by a sinuous snake of stepping stones and the other only admits those willing to undertake a short tricky scramble. Loughrigg Fell itself is a superb objective, with majestic views normally saved for much higher mountains. The extensive summit plateau belies its modest 335m height. The longer route up from the caves has a more wild and adventurous feel than ascending the steep Grasmere flank from Loughrigg Terrace. Opportunities to explore the peaceful shores of Rydal Water and Grasmere are an added bonus to any of the route options.

From **Brant Bows**, follow the dead end road uphill to its end at a gate. Go through this and take the upper of two paths signed to Rydal Cave, rising slightly above **Rydal**

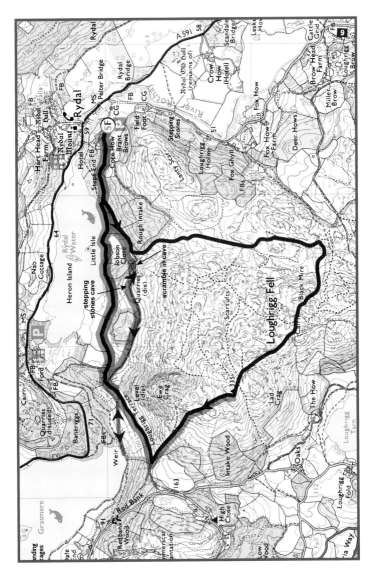

Careful spotting is required for the scramble into the lower cave

Water and traversing the hillside for 500m on a track. After a short rocky and steeper section, cross a stream to reach the lower cave 30m later.

> An easy scramble down leads to a tricky polished 4m climb into the lower quarry cave itself. Many children will need assistance, possibly from an adult at the top and one at the bottom. Before proceeding, be aware that descending is more difficult than going up. There are sometimes bits of fixed rope in situ to aid the scramble into the cave. If in doubt, be content with a visit to the more accessible upper cave. Once inside, the lower cave has a spooky tunnel in the back left corner.

About 60m further up the same path is the upper cave. This is usually flooded and entered by means of a long line of flat and child-friendly stepping stones.

Red option

Good visibility and route-finding skills are needed for this option.

After visiting both caves, double back along the path for 90m to the stream crossing. Take the grassy path going up the left-hand side of the stream.

Go through a distinctive patch of juniper bushes. After 100m take the middle of three paths up through bracken. After around 600m this leads to a large cairn at the top of a small rise. The higher ground of the Loughrigg summit area is visible far to the right. Continue straight ahead, descending slightly. As a wall comes into view 100m to the left, the path forks. Take the right fork heading towards a rocky path running from east to west. Turn right on this path and shortly after cross a stream on a few stepping stones. Here the path splits. Take the right fork heading uphill. By staying on the most walked path and heading for the highest ground (weaving around and over the knobbly summit plateau) the trig point on the highest point of **Loughrigg** is reached after 1km. This section of the route has a very minor scrambling section and commands superb views of Windermere, Elter Water and across to the Langdale fells.

The summit is a scenic perch high above Grasmere. Take the path north-east from the summit heading steeply down towards Grasmere. After about 800m of descending, the path meets a lateral route called **Loughrigg Terrace**, which traverses the hillside above Grasmere. Turn right on this for another 700m until a junction on a shoulder. Taking the higher right-hand path leads back to the caves (passing a good children's bouldering stone halfway along) but follow the lower left-hand fork to descend eventually to the bridleway, which runs along the shores of **Rydal Water**, where there are several beaches and paddling spots. Continue to meet the gate and the outbound route near its start.

A perch high up on Loughrigg

Blue option
In less than perfect visibility, both ascend and descend **Loughrigg** by the **Loughrigg Terrace** route (see the descent of Red option) and come back along the Rydal lake-shore bridleway.

Green option
A great lower level circuit for younger children is to continue along the path from the caves until the junction at the shoulder between Rydal Water and Grasmere. Take the lower right-hand path to descend to **Grasmere lake** near the **weir** and a **beach** a little further on. Retrace your steps to the shoulder, then take the lower left-hand option heading east along the shores of **Rydal Water** to eventually rejoin the out-bound route to the caves where the road ends.

Surprisingly, there are many small fish in the flooded upper Rydal cave.

Bad weather alternative
Stick to the lower level route.

Adventure 8
Castle to castle at Windermere

Cycling from Wray Castle to a mini castle ruin with
opportunities for paddling and swimming

Start/finish	Windermere area. Wray Castle car park (SD 375 010)
Distance	11km (6.8 miles) if you take the blue option or 6km (3.7 miles) if returning by ferry. From 1–7km (0.6–4.3 miles) for the green option.
Suitable for	●● Blue. Children of all ages who can ride a bicycle with control. The green option is entirely traffic-free and easily adaptable to suit the distance needs of younger cyclists.
Amenities	Wray Castle has a café. The lovely Café in the Courtyard is just before the Claife Viewing Station mini castle.
Public transport	The southern end of the route is easily accessed from the Bowness/Windermere ferry
Considerations	The blue route begins with 200m of cycling along the Wray Castle drive (10mph with speed bumps). After 3.5km on the bridleway in the woods, the blue route follows a dead end minor road where walkers and cyclists predominate, though you may meet occasional slow moving vehicles. The green option is traffic-free.

A terrific little cycle ride that reveals the prettier and quieter side of Lake Windermere, this route connects the impressive Wray Castle with the ruined bijou Georgian castle of the Claife Viewing Station. It travels mostly through woods at the edge of the lake. Route finding is easy. The track through the woods undulates with mini hills from time to time, but on the whole the ride is flat and the surface amenable. The route works equally well if started from its southern end.

For the blue route, leave **Wray Castle car park** and follow the drive back to its gate-house. Turn left on the minor road for 30m (dismount if needed) then turn right following a blue signed bridleway to meet the lake at **High Wray Bay**. (The green route accesses High Wray Bay by the footpath south from the car park, but bicycles must be pushed until the bridleway). Continue south along the delightful course of the bridleway, taking care where it passes through a car park after 1km. After 3.5km the

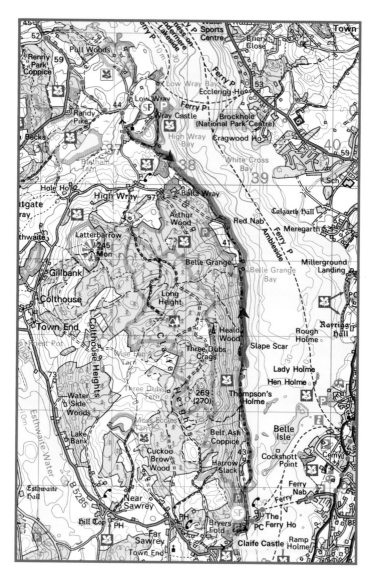

bridleway meets a minor dead end road. The full outbound green route ends here, where there is an open grassy area and a number of small beaches ideal for a picnic and paddle. The blue option continues along the minor road. It rarely has any traffic on it and should be manageable for most families. The Café in the Courtyard with the lower crenulated walls of **Claife Viewing Station** will soon be reached. Leave your bicycles at the café and potter up the path to the curious ruined Georgian Castle.

Claife Castle

Note: Claife Viewing Station is only 250m from 'The Ferry House' terminal. The best route to the ferry terminal avoids the winding B-road, often cluttered with crawling cars, by walking bikes along the signed footpath on the left just before the café. A return ferry journey can be made back from here to the Low Wray Bay landing at Wray Castle, or an excursion made to Bowness on Windermere before the cycle back.

Did you know?

The artist in residence

- Beatrix Potter stayed at Wray Castle on family holidays as a child and fell in love with the Lake District.

- Claife Viewing Station has boards and a sculpture that inform budding young artists about the Picturesque Movement. The Picturesque became popular in the 18th century and has influenced the perception of Lakeland landscapes ever since.

- The most well-known ghost at Wray Castle is that of a phantom white horse and rider. The Claife ferry crossing is also reputedly haunted by a mad monk called the Claife Crier.

Bad weather alternative
Go inside the neo-Gothic Wray Castle (fee/free to NT members) or do the ride anyway.

Adventure 9
Gummer's How and Fell Foot Park

An ideal first fell climb, child-friendly scrambling,
tree climbing and boating

Start/finish	Newby Bridge area. Gummer's How car park (SD 389 877) and Fell Foot National Trust parking (SD 382 869) are signed from the A592.
Distance	2km (1.2 mile) round trip with 140m ascent
Suitable for	● Green. All – babies to grandparents
Amenities	Fell Foot has a café and toilets
Public transport	Bus number 6 to Fell Foot but be warned – the ascent of Gummer's How loses its ease when approached by bus, as it means a hard hike up the road. Just visit Fell Foot instead.
Considerations	Fell Foot Park is close to Gummer's How, but down a steep narrow road. It is best to drive between the two. Parents should be aware that there is a considerable current in the water at the southern end of Fell Foot Park as Windermere eventually becomes the River Leven.

Lakeland fell-walker and author Alfred Wainwright described the miniature beauty of Gummer's How as a saviour for geriatrics. It can also be a breakthrough summit for parents of young or reluctant children. Where Gummer's How is a fun easy excursion for older children, it makes the ideal first 'mountain' challenge for three-year-olds with a strong probability of success. The ascent is scrambly enough to inspire young climbers and make them forget that they want to be carried. Older children can find more exciting rocky passages, which are still comparatively safe. The superb views of Windermere and its tooting Lakeside steam trains give the impression of having gained tremendous heights. Visiting Fell Foot and adding an expedition on the water to explore the true southern end of Windermere makes for a great family day.

Taking the oars at Fell Foot Park

The mighty mini-mountain of Gummer's How

It would be a struggle to get lost on this route. Follow the signed path 50m further up the road from the car park. Take the path, initially through woods onto the heathery open fellside. Keep to the crest and the scrambly chain of easy-angled rocks for the best route to the summit. There is a 3m high natural bouldering wall on the Windermere side of the path near the top that older children may want to test their climbing skills on. From the summit, take a grassy path rightwards away from the lake with small waymarkers. This curves back round past a 'money tree' then a great climbing tree to meet the outbound route.

Fell Foot

Fell Foot Park is owned by the National Trust. It is free to enter but there is paid parking (free for NT members). Double and triple kayaks can be hired in summer, along with traditional four-person rowing boats. It is also very easy to launch your own craft. This is the narrow and quieter foot of Windermere. A good trip manageable in an hour is to head southwards, skirting the promontory to reach the old bridge at Newby Bridge.

Boating at Fell Foot is ideal for waving to steam train passengers, as the Lakeside-Haverthwaite line is very close to the shore.

There is an adventure playground in the park, with a nice little designated tree-climbing area. There are also lakeside barbecue facilities.

Bad weather alternative

Feasible in all conditions. In summer, make the short Fell Foot to Lakeside ferry journey across the lake to the Lakes Aquarium, steam railway and the nearby Lakeland Motor Museum.

Adventure 10
Grizedale Forest – Mushrooms and Wild Art

Traffic free cycling trails, sculpture walks and an adventure playground

Start/finish	Grizedale. Moor Top car park (SD 343 962)
Distance	4km (2.5 miles; longer options available)
Suitable for	● ● The blue main route is manageable for most younger cyclists. The red, harder and longer option is 11km (6.8 miles). There are walking trails for all ages.
Amenities	Café, bike hire and toilets at Grizedale visitor centre 2.5km down the road from Moor Top.
Considerations	Although the main route is by far the flattest cycling trail at Grizedale, there are still some hilly sections and children on single speed bikes may have to push on a couple of sections.

Grizedale is an immense forest with reputedly more than four million trees. It's famous for its collection of around 50 weird and wonderful sculptures, which are spaced out around the park so that a smattering are visible on most of the walking and cycling trails. Owing to the fellside location of the forest, most of the cycling trails are pretty tough for children; the Goosey Foot Tarn Trail and Mushroom Trail are happy exceptions. Both start north of the busy main activity hub at the visitor centre at the high Moor Top car park where the forest feels more untamed. These trails take wide forest roads with decent surfaces and colourful wooden mushroom sculptures to find on route. By combining a ride far into the woods, exploring some forest sculpture culture and perhaps visiting the adventure playground, Grizedale is a good family outing.

Goosey Foot Tarn Trail is well waymarked with blue arrows. Go up the main track from the car park for a short distance before turning left to do the loop in the better clock-wise direction. This swings past Juniper Tarn (one of 20 manmade tarns in the forest), which is just visible through the trees. The route bears sharply right at an open area with a mushroom on the bend where there is a gradual climb. Follow markers keeping right at the remaining track junctions, passing Goosey Foot Tarn (hidden through

Tackling one of the climbs on the Goosey Foot Tarn Trail

trees to your left) on a lovely flat section. The ride concludes with a long gradual descent back to the car park.

The longer Mushroom Trail is designed as a children's bike orienteering course. Five mushrooms are passed on the Goosey Foot Trail but the longer route visits 11. Get a special map from the visitor centre and plot a course to find the mushrooms, count the spots, crack a code and return to collect a sticker from the visitor centre (as the centre is not located at the end of the route, staff will happily give parents a sticker in advance).

Mea Culpa sculpture on the Bogle Crag trail

Maps

We have not included OS mapping for this route. A more suitable map is available free online at www.forestry.gov.uk/pdf/MTBz-foldinteriorp1(A3).pdf or alternatively search 'Grizedale cycling map'. All the cycling trails apart from the orienteering route of the Mushroom Trail are included. For maps of the walking trails go to www.forestry.gov.uk/pdf/WalkingLeafletContent.pdf or search 'Grizedale walking map'. For a sculpture key go to: www.forestryengland.uk/grizedale/cycling-and-moun-tain-biking-trails and then click on the map link at the bottom of the page.

Alternative routes

There are other longer and more challenging biking options for older children such as the Grizedale Tarn Trail (10km from the Bogle Crag car park at SD 338 932). Impressive sculptures such as *Mea Culpa* by Robert Bryce Muir or *Taking a Wall for a Walk* by Andy Goldsworthy can be visited on route. Also from the Bogle Crag car park, the 5km Bogle Crag walking trail takes in these and other sculptures and is a worthwhile route for non-cyclists.

There are mountain biking routes at Grizedale but most under 12s (and most parents too) would find them excessively challenging.

At the visitor centre, walking and cycling maps are available. Family bike hire, including child trailers, is also available although be aware that the easier cycle trails starting from the centre are quite difficult and arguably somewhat monotonous for younger children. Cycling up from here to the recommended trail at Moor Top is quite strenuous. A more gradual off-road trail linking the two car parks is planned.

Bad weather alternative

The forest is not unpleasant in bad weather as it is mainly sheltered and the visitor centre and café provide places to dry off.

Not for lunch – poisonous looking looking mushroom in Grizedale Forest

Adventure 11
Hampsfell and its curious Hospice

Exploring the weird and wonderful 'Hospice', climbing
a small fell and child friendly scrambling

Start/finish	Cartmel. Roadside parking at the junction of Fell End Road and the Grange – Cartmel Spring Bank Road (SD 395 778).
Distance	4km (2.5 mile) round trip with 100m ascent
Suitable for	● Green. All ages. Easy terrain underfoot.
Amenities	Grange-over-Sands
Public transport	Grange-over-Sands train station is 1 mile from the start of the route. There are pleasant connecting paths from here up to the main route through Charney Well and down through Eggerslack Woods.
Considerations	Younger children need close supervision on the open stone steps and the hospice platform.

The mini summit of Hampsfell lies in solitary splendour in the very southernmost reaches of the Lake District National Park. Its lack of crowds, gradual grassy slopes and quirky features make it an ideal adventure for families with children of all ages. There is a substantial swathe of limestone pavement on the fell-top, perfect for children to explore. The 'Hospice' also provides an appealing and unusual destination, with its wooden viewfinder, bizarre staircase and old inscriptions and riddles. The panoramic view includes Morecambe Bay, the Kent viaduct, the Howgills and Yorkshire's Three Peaks, as well as the higher Lakeland fells.

Walk up the dead end Fell End Road for 50m. Turn left at a signpost onto the slopes of **Fell End**. Here, take the middle path, climbing past two obvious large boulders, which provide some good scrambling opportunities. The route soon becomes less steep, passing several windblown trees and a rocky area with a small den before veering leftwards to reach the cairned top of **Fell End**. From here, the ridge line path is followed as it dips slightly to cross a stile and then rises to the visible hospice on top of **Hampsfell**. The clints (protruding bits) and grikes (channels) of the limestone paving are visible all over the summit area, with the most extensive part

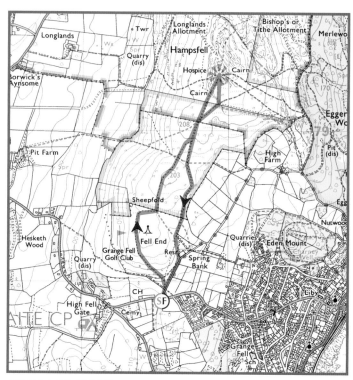

An itchy sheep at one of the beautiful windblown trees on route

Hampsfell Hospice: investigating the limestone paving

to the north. It is possible to return by different paths, keeping a little further east and not visiting Fell End.

Bad weather alternative
Viable in bad weather, take shelter in the hospice. Bring a stove and make hot chocolate.

Did you know?

- The Greek inscription at the hospice means 'rosy-fingered dawn' and probably refers to the Greek goddess Eos who opened the gates of heaven to let the dawn light in each morning.

- The viewfinder on the hospice's platform is called an alidade. It can be used to accurately locate some Lakeland landmarks.

- Hampsfell Hospice was built in 1846 by the vicar of nearby Cartmel to provide shelter for passing travellers. There are several riddles and rhyming warnings on plaques inside the hospice.

- Blackberries can be harvested on the summit plateau in season.

Adventure 12
Hodbarrow Lagoon and Haverigg lighthouses

Biking to a deserted beach, sandcastle building, scrambling,
bird-watching and visiting lighthouse ruins

Start/finish	Haverigg. Parking area just before the entrance to Port Haverigg caravan site at (SD 164 787).
Distance	5.6km (3.5 miles)
Suitable for	● Green. All ages. Young cyclists should be able to manage this flat ride, though some surfaces are quite bumpy. It is also great as a walk.
Amenities	Haverigg has toilets, a playground, pubs, a chip shop and a café. Port Haverigg caravan site has a shop, bar, café and a small watersports centre.
Public transport	Millom station provides a rail link 1.5km north of the route.
Considerations	Do not walk out onto the mud flats of the Duddon Estuary. Bring binoculars, buckets and spades. Closely supervise children on the rocky part of the beach if the tide is coming in. As parts of the route are on a byway, it is possible that cyclists might meet a slow vehicle. Another section goes through a caravan site (speed bumps and 5mph limit).

Ssshhh...keep this one to yourselves. Few Lakeland visitors ever make it to this
superb coastal nature reserve. Fewer still find its beautiful secret sandy beach. The
unassuming village of Haverigg is just 3 miles south of the national park boundary.
This route uses a gravel byway to circumnavigate the Hodbarrow Nature Reserve,
managed by the RSPB. There are expansive views south across the Duddon Sands
over the Irish Sea and northwards to Scafell and the Old Man of Coniston. The
ride is the perfect length for children, with plenty to stop and see: two disused
lighthouses, one ruined windmill, a public bird hide and an impressive sea wall
all embellish the route. These attractions will pale in comparison to the beach at
Hodbarrow Point. Swimming is not advised, but paddling and making good use
of the perfect castle-constructing sand is recommended. There are rock pools
to explore and a wonderful expanse of easy-angled limestone, which is the ideal
spot for young scramblers.

Haverigg Lighhouse

Follow the byway sign at the side of the **caravan site** entrance. This takes you to the right, away from the site onto a long, arcing spit with the unusual lagoon on the left and sea on the right. Continue on the narrower path to the right of a larger track (vehicles *are* permitted to come down this track, although few ever risk wrecking their axles on the horrendously potholed surface). After just over a mile this reaches **Haverigg Lighthouse**, behind which the outer barrier of the sea wall can be inspected. Take care if you allow your children to explore the tempting looking angled blocks as they have deep, leg-sized gaps between them. Opposite the lighthouse, the **building with bird-themed murals** is a public hide overlooking the lagoon. It has information about which birds can be seen (there are flocks upon flocks of them).

A further 900m brings you to **Hodbarrow Point**. Leave the bikes and follow one of several paths a short way down to the **beach**. There is plenty to explore for

Scouring the rock pools of the 'secret' beach

Riding to the beach and the ruined windmill at Hodbarrow Point

Popping out of a smuggler's cave through the rocks at Hodbarrow Point

all ages here: tons of scrambling, rock pools and grassy paths on the headland. The grassy hummocks above the beach are home to a ruined **windmill** and the site of an old **quarry**.

From the sign and bench on the byway by the beach, turn left towards another visible old lighthouse. Pass by this (the easiest way up to its base is behind it) and continue on the eastern side of the lagoon. The byway then runs alongside the track once again and eventually the byway joins a tarmacked section of track. Continue on this for a very short section, going straight ahead just before the caravan site's back entrance on a more overgrown section of the byway. This emerges on the site and the last 500m stretch back to the start of the route. Caravan site vehicles can travel at 5mph along this stretch. There are speed bumps but take care with younger children.

> At Hodbarrow Point, there is a hidden 'smugglers' barrel' that a storm tide has washed up improbably into a vertical cave in the back of the most defined inlet in the rocks on the beach. Lithe urchins may even be able to squeeze up behind this to emerge at the top of the rocks.

Bad weather alternative
Feasible in bad weather as a walk to the first lighthouse taking shelter in the hide.

Did you know?

- Iron was mined on Hodbarrow in the first half of the 20th century. The outer sea wall was completed in 1905 after two unsuccessful attempts to protect the mine from the ravages of the tides. The mine was once one of the most productive in the world. When it closed in 1968, the saltwater lagoon formed as the land subsided.

Adventure 13

Stickle Pike – a big mountain in miniature

Climbing a mini-mountain, scrambling, exploring
quarries, cairn building and rare bird spotting

Start/finish	Seathwaite area. Layby parking at the top of Kiln Bank Cross (NY 214 933). Reached from Broughton Mills or Hall Bridge near Seathwaite.
Distance	2.5km (1.6 miles) and 130m height gain, with optional extension activities.
Suitable for	● Green. Children of all ages.
Considerations	The road up from Broughton Mills is gated. Take care if exploring the old quarry workings and tunnels.

A magical little outing to inspire budding young fell walkers, the little-known Stickle Pike is one of the finest mini-summits in the Lake District. Its two airy tops allow stunning views south to Duddon Sands, the Irish Sea and, on clear days, Snowdonia, while to the north there is a superb panorama of high Lakeland fells. If tackled from the pass at the top of Kiln Bank Cross, Stickle Pike has the character of a high Lakeland peak achieved with only a fraction of the usual ascent. There is a small reedy tarn to relax at on the way down. The outing is easily extended by exploring the amenably-angled scrambling rocks on the opposite side of the road and continuing to the quarry workings where an old tunnel can be ventured into (wet floor, torch needed) and perhaps one of Britain's rarest birds might be spotted. This area is also a good location for children to try their hand at cairn building or kite flying.

From the parking area, cross the road and follow the right-hand broad path uphill. This splits at a shoulder. Take the left fork that leads pleasantly up the steep western edge of the fell. Stay on the well-worn path winding up to the obvious cairned summit – another airy sister peak a little farther along is worth popping to. After admiring the views from the summit, a steep scree-ridden path can be taken down to **Stickle Tarn** just off the descent path. However, it is easier to retrace your

In summer, bright blue damselfly dragonflies and various butterflies flutter to and fro at the tarn.

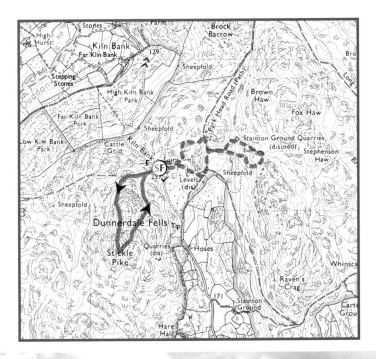

A lofty perch for young alpinists atop Stickle Pike

Let's go fly a kite
at Kiln Bank Cross

ascent route for 80m or so to a mini col where a less awkward faint grassy path can be followed to the tarn. From the tarn follow the descent path back to the parking area.

Optional extensions
On the opposite side of the road to **Stickle Pike**, myriad paths weave among the craggy hillocks and quarry workings, which are ideal for mini scrambles and hide-and-seek. Follow the signed bridleway eastwards for 150m until a well-built **cairn** can be spotted to your left. Children can try their hand at cairn building here or near the quarry. Head up past the large cairn, and follow the hilltop until a clear path leads down rightwards to join another. Descend this for 100m, then branch left to follow a path towards the large quarry. A dark tunnel can be explored just down the hillside from the **quarry**. It appears stable enough – but you enter at your own risk.

The large quarry with its jumble of fallen blocks obviously requires caution. Its rocks have been known to host rare birds – a sunken twitcher's hide can found on the precipitous hillside (with care). Another quarry working farther up the hill has an interesting narrow cleft to explore.

Adventure 14
Kail Pot and Hardnott Roman Fort

Paddling and swimming, a short walk and exploration
of the Roman ruins of Hardnott Castle

Start/finish	Eskdale area. Parking at SD 213 012 for Kail Pot and SD 220 214 for the fort. Best approached from Ravenglass via Dunnerdale to avoid the often stressful drive over Hardknott and Wrynose Passes.
Distance	3.2km (2 miles)
Suitable for	⬤ Blue. Little height gain and mainly on steady paths (longer blue extension possible). Quite an adventurous pool not suitable for the very youngest paddlers.
Amenities	The closest are the café at Dalegarth Station and pubs in Eskdale and Boot.
Public transport	The Ravenglass and Eskdale steam railway to Dalegarth Station is 4km away.
Considerations	Extra close supervision should be given to children at the gorge and pool of Kail Pot where there are rocky drops. As with any stream or river swimming, depths and currents should be checked – particularly after heavy rains. Wetsuits recommended.

Wild swimming where the Esk falls into Kail Pot and slows through an enchanted twin-sectioned pool is simply delightful. Children will love immersing themselves in what is surely the clearest water in the Lake District – no goggles required here! A little 'you'll get used to it' coaxing may be needed – these waters flow off of England's highest mountains after all – but the entry area is shallow and ideal for paddlers to build up to braving a little swim. Adults can stand up in both pools, making this a relatively straightforward spot to manage young swimmers. Combining the swimming with a visit to the scenically located second century Hardnott Castle (the Roman Fort of *Mediobogdum*), where the ghosts of centurions guard one of the most famous passes in Britain, is certain to interest budding archaeologists.

Checking the perimeter at Hardknott Fort

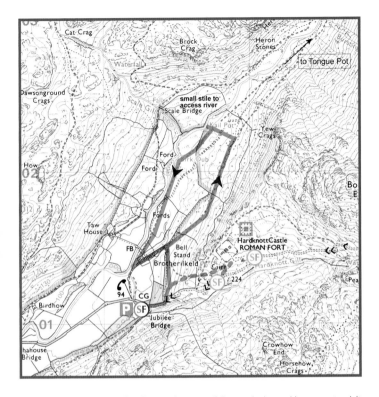

Most parties will visit the fort first. Park at one of the two layby parking areas to visit the **fort** (information boards here), then drive down to the larger parking area among trees near the western foot of the pass in order to avoid a steep return hike after swimming. From the parking area in the trees, walk 30m uphill. Turn left and follow the wall to cross a ladder stile. Alternatively, the energetic can leave a car at the lower of the two fort parking areas and, after visiting the ruins, follow the path south west down the hill, passing over a stile and continuing steeply to join the primary route after the ladder stile.

After 300m the path is joined by another coming from the farm. Head north-east up the valley, passing a good boulder for scrambling. Continue through two gates and, 100m before a third wall, strike left downhill towards the river. Locate a small stile over the fence to reach **Kail Pot**. Access to the pool requires a little scramble down a stepped ramp to a shallow area.

Braving a swim in the cool mountain waters at Kail Pot

There is another slightly larger and deeper pool with a bigger waterfall about 80m upstream, but the current is strong and access is much more difficult.

Other good pools and paddling areas can be found upstream – Tongue Pot is 2km further upstream along the same path and Esk Falls 300m further still. From here it is possible to walk back on a path along the other side of the stream, making the whole route 7.5km.

Cross back over the stile and turn right to follow the path running parallel to the Esk downstream. Look out for a superb little hiding place under some tree roots on the way back. As you reach the farm, watch out for a path on the left before a tiny bridge: this avoids most of the farmyard. Pass through a gate and follow the track for 100m or so until heading right returns you to the stile and parking area.

Did you know?

- The dramatically situated Hardknott Fort was built under the rule of Roman Emperor Hadrian, who also built the famous wall. The fort had its own bath-house and parade ground.

- The road over Hardknott Pass was also originally built by the Romans. Now the narrow twisting road with its famous 1-in-3 gradient challenges drivers with steep hairpin bends and is a testpiece for committed cyclists.

Adventure 15
Ride the Esk Trail to the sea

Off road biking, a steam train trip, paddling and a coastal finale

Start	Boot in Eskdale. The car park (donation) (NY 172 003) at the end of a minor road which leaves the Eskdale road 350m south-west of Dalegarth Station.
Finish	Ravenglass
Distance	14km (8.7 miles) for full ride (shorter variations possible)
Suitable for	● Red. Competent and energetic young cyclists. Shorter turnaround options with a picnic on the river can be equally rewarding for younger children. Reaching the golf course clubhouse café (cyclists welcome) just before the steep hill is another option.
Amenities	Café and toilets at Dalegarth and Ravenglass
Public transport	Ravenglass and Eskdale Railway links the start and finish points of the route. If you have booked ahead you can take bikes on the steam train to Dalegarth Station in order to begin the ride and park there.
Considerations	Entry level mountain biking on a child-friendly surface: there are no steep drops. Areas where dismounts are needed are obvious. The main climb requires a bike push. The route is virtually traffic free: there is a 300m passage on an exceptionally minor road. Cyclists should dismount for the crossing of the A595 at Muncaster Castle.

This superb linear ride starts among a cradle of craggy heather-dressed Lakeland hills and wends its way to the open panorama of the Irish Sea at Ravenglass. It has all the best ingredients for a classic children's adventure amid varied scenery, and is not to be missed. The route has sections of manageable challenge – including one bike-push up a steep hill – interspersed with long passages on easier terrain. For budding young wheelers who can cover a few miles on a bicycle, cycle comfortably over grass or muddy paths in the park and make it happily along farm tracks, this is the perfect next step.

The steam railway can be used to return to Dalegarth Station from Ravenglass (you must book ahead with bikes). Taking a bike lock and picking the bikes up later by car is also a good solution. For parties with one car and two adults,

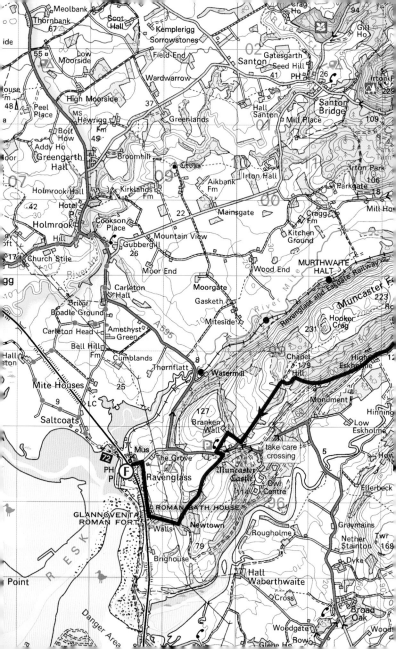

another option is to reach Ravenglass and, while the kids enjoy a well-deserved break at the coast, one adult reverses the route to retrieve the car.

Leave the parking area and turn left up the track, reaching a gate after 100m or so. Pass through the gate. Here, a short bumpy incline will cause most cyclists to dismount – don't be perturbed, things soon improve. At the top of the incline, you will intercept the Esk Trail. Turn right on this through an open meadow and enter woods. The trail, which is now well-signed and easily followed, weaves its way beside the Esk.

After 3km, you'll cross a cattle grid and, shortly afterwards, meet a road at **Forge Bridge**. The road is quiet, wide and open, so easily cycled by most families. Turn left for 300m until a right turn at **Forge House** farm leads you back off-road. The track is generally now much easier to cycle along and good progress can be made.

High Eskholme Farm golf course has a cafe that welcomes cyclists.

Just beyond **High Eskholme Farm**, the Esk Trail leaves the valley floor rightwards and heads up a steep climb. Unquestionably this is the hardest part of the route. A demoralising bike push up the hill is needed. However, the trudge has exceptional pay-offs and parents will be encouraged to know that from the top of the climb the remaining cycle to Ravenglass is on steady terrain that is either on relatively gradual down-hills or flat and well-surfaced.

From the gate at the top of the main ascent, bicycles can be remounted. Follow the path as it climbs gently to the high point of the route – a T-junction with a track (**Fell Lane**) beside a tarn. Turn left here. Soon afterwards the Irish Sea makes a surprising and spectacular appearance. Follow Fell Lane straight down the hill. Just as

The magnificent Esk Trail with Caw beyond

The Irish Sea making its surprise appearance on the Esk Trail

you reach the A595 a sharp right turn is taken on another track. Follow this, swinging left after 150m and continue until meeting the A595. Dismount to cross the road and enter the grounds of **Muncaster Castle**. The Esk Trail is signposted on a right turn just before the ticket office and this is followed with ease through the estate.

After you pass **Decoy Pond**, bear right on the signed trail towards the well-surfaced track and the red sandstone remains of Glannaventa Roman bathhouse, also known as **Walls Castle**.

> The Roman bathhouse of Walls Castle belonged to a Roman fort built around 130AD. It is the starting point for the fantastic 174-mile Hadrian's Cycle Way, which works up the Cumbrian coast, follows Hadrian's Wall and ends at the surprising remains of Arbeia Roman Fort at Tynemouth in South Shields.

Continue along the track. A footpath on the left just before the road allows the **steam railway station** to be accessed – this has a café and a gift shop. There is a pub on the platform of the main railway at **Ravenglass** – the Ratty Arms, and two or three more inns on the quiet main street. The mud and sand beach is a good place to look for wrecks.

Bad weather alternative
Take the steam train ride or visit Muncaster Castle.

Adventure 16
The Fickle Steps of Dunnerdale

Crossing the River Duddon by unusual stepping stones, hiking, scrambling and paddling

Start/finish	Seathwaite area. Small parking area on the Duddon Valley road 2km north of Seathwaite (NY 232 975).
Distance	4.5km (2.8 miles) or 1km (0.6 miles)
Suitable for	● ● Blue with shorter green option
Amenities	Seathwaite has a pub which sells ice cream, teas and food.
Considerations	Some steep and narrow paths and drops to the river. In damp conditions, the rock can be very slippery. A section of walking on a very quiet road.

The Fickle Steps are just that – in dry conditions many young children will whizz across the stepping stones with their cable handrail. Conversely, in high water or after wet weather the steps can be a slippery foot-soaking challenge. Children will enjoy exploring the rocky bed of the River Duddon, where there is an even trickier set of stepping stones for those who found the Fickle Steps too tame. The second part of the route passes through open land on the other side of remote Dunnerdale and few who visit will not want to return to this remarkably quiet corner of the national park.

Go west down the marked path from the parking spot, which descends to reach the **Fickle Steps** after 300m. If the stones are impassable simply revert to the green option (described below).

After crossing the stones, turn left on the path heading downstream. Go through a wall then turn right to gain some height and negotiate a steep sided bank of the **river**. Take care here where there is a short section on a fairly narrow path above a steep slope. The path then descends back to the river (although it feels as if it is taking you away from it).

Continue following the river for a further 800m. Along its course there are several large boulders which provide good scrambling opportunities and two islands that it may be possible to clamber on to depending on water conditions. The rock scenery of the riverbed is always interesting. Cross the river on a distinctive slender stone bridge. Turn immediately right to discover a second set of **stepping stones**

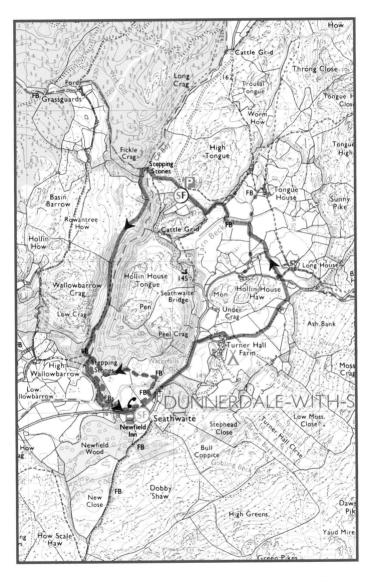

after 50m. The route does not cross these but children will want to negotiate them in dry conditions. They provide a stiffer challenge than the neighbouring Fickle Steps.

Continue downstream on the most walked path to reach a tributary and another footbridge, which leads into **Seathwaite**. The Duddon is shallower and wider here with plenty of good paddling, scrambling and skimming potential. Turn left and walk along the very quiet road into the hamlet. Take a path left (roughly opposite the pub) through a couple of fields to cut off a small corner and rejoin the road. Continue up the road for 400m then turn right up the track to Turner Hall farm and campsite. At the first bend, leave the track on a path going left through fields. Here, there is a rocky knoll that provides a few scrambling opportunities for younger children. Stay left of a lonely house to reach a tiny dead end road. Continue on a path straight across this down beside a wall. At a track turn right then take a footpath left alongside a stream to cross a footbridge. Skirt the field rightwards (the path has been rerouted due to habitual flooding) then go left at the top of the field to reach a stile. Cross this and go straight up the path to reach the **parking area** where you started.

Bad weather alternative

Following the green option, take the path opposite the pub in **Seathwaite**. Instead of rejoining the road, turn left and then swing round leftwards to meet the **stepping stones** with the footbridge after 500m. Turn left and follow the main route back into Seathwaite.

Did you know?

- There are no less than seven sets of stepping stones on the Duddon between Ulpha and Cockley Beck – surely some kind of record! It could be a challenge to cross them all.
- There are several other great paddling/picnicking spots upstream of Seathwaite at Birk's Bridge and Froth Pot.

Negotiating the Fickle Steps

Running wild amid the bluebells

Enjoying a three-course dinner: the starter (bottom right), the main course (top) and the Pudding Stone (bottom left)

Adventure 17
Meet the Old Man of Coniston

Climbing a famous high mountain with mining history, scrambling and optional youth hostelling

Start/finish	Coniston area. Walna Scar car park (SD 289 970)
Distance	8km (5 miles); 5.5km (3.4 miles) shorter route. 600m ascent to the summit.
Suitable for	● Red (the summit there-and-back route is easier but still red). This is one of the simpler high fells to tackle. Low Water makes a good destination in itself (blue, 4km, 250m ascent) and is a good spot for tired family members to wait for a summit party.
Amenities	Coniston has a good range of refreshments and toilets.
Public transport	Bus 505 goes to Coniston from Ambleside. Starting from Coniston is a longer but still feasible hike for older children. Follow signs for the Old Man from the village centre leading up the left side of Church Beck to join the main route at the first junction after 2.5km.
Considerations	CAUTION: Some of the boulders in Boulder Valley have high drops off one side. Pay close attention – these scrambles are graded red. Wait for dry conditions. Adults should check the scrambles first. Walna Scar road is extremely steep – avoid driving it if icy.

The Old Man is high, mighty and rugged and has a fascinating story to tell. The 803m peak has long captured the imaginations of adults and children. Its steep-flanked tarns, curving ridges, craggy faces and boulder-strewn slopes make it a tantalising objective. The scars of slate and copper mining on the mountain make for a summit hike where there is always something interesting to see. The relative altitude of the Walna Scar car park means that the Old Man's lofty crown is an achievable objective for many children, though some may only get as far as the superb mountainside paddling spots at Low Water and some may get to the summit and come down the same way. For tough young walkers, the full route gives the opportunity to explore the peaceful northern reaches of the Old Man at Levers Water and the scrambling challenges of the Pudding Stone and its near neighbours.

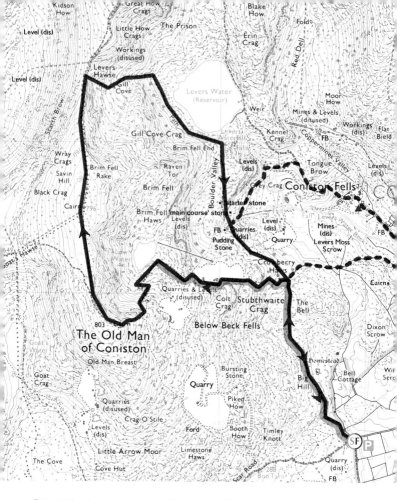

From Walna Scar car park, take the track heading north beside a wall at first. This rises gently, quickly gaining views of **Coniston Water**, for 2km to a shoulder just past the craggy top of **The Bell**. Here, the track swings round leftwards and is joined by another well-used path. After 50m, take the left-hand fork and the track now climbs steeply past **Colt Crag** to the disused remnants of the historic slate-mining operations on the fell. There is still some rail track, cogs and cabling along the route and children can easily imagine how the slate was cut and then transported down the

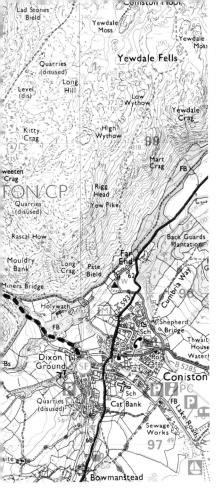

mountainside. There are several old slate-built **quarry buildings** and a short tunnel to find. This area is deemed an industrial archaeology site and artefacts are not to be removed. From the flat area of slate quarry buildings, there is a great view of the Coppermines Valley with the scars and spoil heaps of its copper mining.

The track continues to climb steeply up to the dramatically cupped tarn of **Low Water**. There are plenty of boulders to clamber on here and good paddling spots further rightwards along the water's edge.

From Low Water, the path continues up the striking ridge to the left all the way to the summit plateau. It's a steep climb and may take you more than an hour.

At the top, it is easy to retrace your steps. If you have a little more time and energy, continue on the ridge path north. The circular route is well worth doing to explore an unfrequented and wilder side of the mountain. Descend a little and then climb again slightly to reach a **cairn** after 750m. Descend gently for a further 1km and then more steeply to a col at **Levers Hawse**. Just before the path starts to climb again, look out for a fainter path descending rightwards quite steeply at first. Take this, the path becoming more distinct and rocky as it descends. Follow the line of **Cove Beck** down to the reservoir of **Levers Water** – a much less frequented paddling stop. The path trends rightwards above Levers Water, climbing slightly to a fenced off area above a rift in the rock. Continue rightwards and south up the fence line over a shoulder into **Boulder Valley**. The path descends through the aptly named valley. Children may suddenly get a second wind here as there are numerous excellent scrambling opportunities on the boulders, which seem to increase in size as the valley descends.

Arctic explorer at Low Water on a winter visit to the Old Man

The most exciting of all the boulders in Boulder Valley is the Pudding Stone, a gigantic Christmas pudding shaped lump which looks unassailable from the approach over a footbridge. It is possible, with care and bone-dry conditions, to shepherd older children up the obvious runnel on the back side. Younger children may content themselves with climbing either the 'starter' stone 200m back along the upper side of the path, or the 'main course' stone (a wedged-shaped boulder between the two on the lower side of the path).

Continue straight ahead on the path traversing the hillside above the Coppermines Valley. This meets the outbound route after 1km. Retrace your steps back to the car park.

Alternative red route

The **Coppermines youth hostel** is a great adventurous place to stay. If you start from here, follow the quarry track uphill beside **Levers Water Beck**. Cross the beck on a footbridge after 800m and continue on the path traversing the head of the valley to join the path from Boulder Valley at the bridge by the **Pudding Stone**.

Bad weather alternatives

Not a good choice in bad weather.

Did you know?

- The Old Man appears as 'Kanchenjunga' in Arthur Ransome's *Swallows and Amazons* series. The real Kanchenjunga is the world's third highest mountain and can be found in the Himalayas.

Adventure 18
Pavey Ark and Stickle Ghyll scramble

Scrambling up to a lofty tarn and hiking over a high mountain, paddling

Start/finish	Great Langdale. Stickle Ghyll paid National Trust car park (NY 295 064.)
Distance	The full route is 6.5km (4 miles) with 620m ascent. To Stickle Tarn and back is 3km (1.9 miles) with 500m ascent.
Suitable for	● Red – older children and parents with scrambling experience and navigation skills.
Amenities	Toilets in car park. Pub and café in Great Langdale.
Public transport	Bus 516 from Ambleside
Considerations	CAUTION: Stickle Ghyll involves grade 1 scrambling. In essence, this is entry level rock climbing without ropes. It is imperative parents understand the risks inherent in grade 1 scrambling and gain prior experience before considering this activity. A one-adult-to-one-child ratio is advised. The level of the stream and the dryness of the rock beside it need to be considered. It is best tackled on a hot, dry day after a period of settled weather..

Generations of youngsters and adults alike have had their first experience of proper scrambling on the slabby rock of Stickle Ghyll. It is a tremendously fun scramble that offers a pleasing alternative to the otherwise steep approach to Stickle Tarn – one of the Lakes' most scenic spots. A scramble to suit age and ability should be easy to fashion as Stickle Ghyll is always escapable and amenable ways of tackling or avoiding its various obstacles can be found without difficulty. There are ample good hand and foot holds and parents should be able to protect children where necessary. The gill leads straight up to the enticing waters of Stickle Tarn, from where a little further effort can take you to the rocky ridge line and to the knobbly 700m high vantage point of Pavey Ark – one of the famous Langdale Pikes.

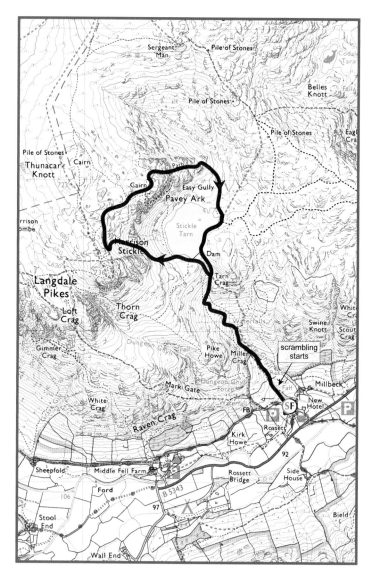

Note: Do not be perturbed by outdoor groups clad in wetsuits; there is no reason to actively seek out wet steps and plunge pools – unless you particularly want to get a soaking. That said, the amount of water in the gill will affect the line and there is little doubt that it is best undertaken during dry spells.

Leave the car park by the path at its top left corner and head up parallel to and on the left of the gill. The path draws close to the gill at a particularly steep waterfall section. Most parties wisely choose to dodge this difficult step and the gill is best joined shortly afterwards. Thereafter tackle obstacles to suit, remembering that not everything should be climbed direct and easier alternatives or bypasses are usually found on the left – where an escape from the gill is also always possible. A wire fence halfway up necessitates a short detour left uphill to a stile. After a fantastic crescendo on quality stepped slabs, the scrambling peters out and the main path on the left of the gill to the tarn's **dam** is followed.

Stickle Tarn has pebbly beaches and is a good place for a picnic, paddling or skimming stop.

Adventure 18 – Pavey Ark and Stickle Ghyll scramble   111

The vertiginous cliffs of Pavey Ark form the immediate backdrop to **Stickle Tarn**. From the dam, follow the path around the left side of the tarn for 150m, then head uphill on a cairned path towards the ridgeline. This eventually reaches a very large cairn on top of a big rectangular boulder. Thirty metres beyond this, turn right at a T-junction in the path and follow a cairned traversing line towards the summit of **Pavey Ark**. The path weaves through rocky terrain and crosses a small wall near the summit of the peak. Pavey Ark summit is unmarked but has some lovely rough rocks to scramble on.

Head north from the summit to intercept a clear and cairned path that is followed back down to the opposite side of Stickle Tarn. A choice of paths beginning on either side of the gill can be used for the descent. The most well-maintained path begins on the west side before crossing to the east side.

Warning: The dotted 'path' marked on OS maps dissecting the cliffs of Pavey Ark is not a path at all but Jack's Rake, an exposed grade 1 scramble that works up a distinctive ramp with steep sections. It has seen fatalities in recent years and has been deemed inadvisable for children. 'Easy Gully', which is also marked on the OS map, is dangerous and loose.

Adventure 19
A wild Ennerdale journey to Black Sail

Biking along forest tracks to reach a remote youth hostel, paddling in a mountain river

Start/finish	Ennerdale Bridge area. Park at Bowness Knott (NY 109 153).
Distance	19km (11.8 miles) for the full ride with 230m ascent (mainly on the outbound ride), but it's possible to turn around at any point.
Suitable for	● ● Main route is red, suitable for confident cyclists on bikes with gears. All families can manage some of the route at green – the initial forest track is suitable for pushchairs, balance bikes etc.
Amenities	Ennerdale YHA café and Black Sail YHA honesty box system and toilets.
Considerations	Although this whole route is designated as traffic-free, guests using the youth hostel at High Gillerthwaite are allowed to drive up the first part of the track. Farm and forestry workers and the wardens of Black Sail hostel use the whole outbound route so be prepared to meet the occasional vehicle – it's not quite as remote as the internet hype would have you believe. The gravel track is loose in places and children must have decent bike handling skills before embarking on the longer ride. Similarly, the ride is viable but not easy for adults with child seats/trailers. The last 300m of the full route to Black Sail is on harder terrain and most families will prefer to leave their bikes at the gate just prior to the hostel. The return journey is much easier.

Ennerdale Water is a far-flung and relatively little-visited lake with a valley only accessible by car from the west. The forestry road network makes for excellent cycling with superb views of Pillar Rock and Great Gable, initially along the peaceful shores of Ennerdale Water, where there are ample paddling and picnicking spots. Those with the stamina to venture beyond the head of the lake and High Gillerthwaite youth hostel's café will find a more secluded but well-made track beside and above the River Liza to the stunningly located and iconic Black Sail hostel at the far edge of the fell-side plantations where the high mountains of Haystacks, Great Gable and Kirk Fell form a shapely head to the valley. Black Sail stays open during the day with refreshments available on an honesty box basis. It makes an unforgettable stop and alternative tracks back down the southern side of the River Liza give one of the best longer family cycling routes in the whole national park.

The track descends fairly steeply to the **lake** from beyond the car park gate – take care here and note that many children will have to push their bikes back up this on the return route. The track then follows the shoreline passing a number of lovely prom-ontories with picnic benches and paddling beaches with a few short ups and downs. The end of the lake at **Char Dub** is gained with surprising ease. Here, the beach by a concrete bridge over the ingress of the **River Liza** makes a good turnaround/ paddle

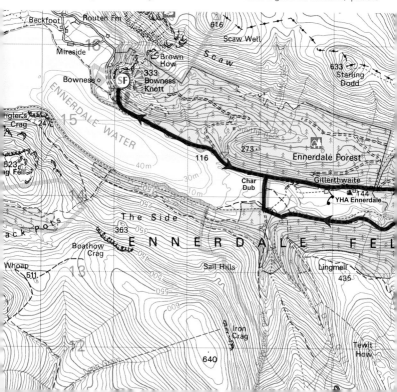

stop for younger riders. Continue, gaining a little height, for 1.2km to reach Ennerdale YHA hostel with its seasonal café. It is a further 5km to Black Sail. As the track climbs above the Liza there are spectacular views of **Pillar Rock** to the right and eventually the craggy north face of Great Gable. The track stays well above the river to gain a gate where the eagle-eyed will glimpse the stone building at **Black Sail**. Leave the bikes here and walk the last 300m to the hostel, which is kindly left open providing shelter, hot drinks, flapjacks, games and even guitars to make a unique stop for passers-by.

Retrace your steps to the gate and take the track descending leftwards through another gate and then a rideable concrete ford over the Liza. The track, which has a less bumpy surface than the outbound route, is grassy at first. It soon swings round rightwards and becomes stonier, passing a large erratic boulder after 1.5km. A long gradual descent to a bridge follows. This is another excellent paddling/swimming/scrambling spot in low water. Don't cross, but continue slightly uphill to cross a tributary with a waterfall and a second stream then descend to a flatter lovely riverside plain. Go through a gate and across a narrower wooden bridge then swing right to cross the **Char Dub concrete bridge** and regain the outbound route.

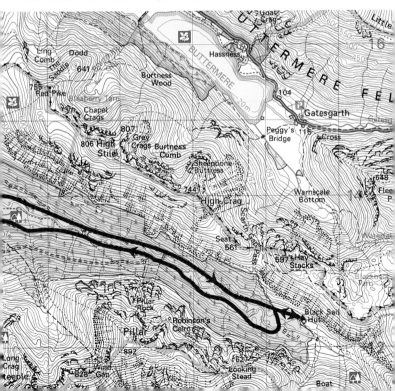

Bursting into song amid the inspiring surroundings at Black Sail

The lakeshore forestry road with the high fells of Steeple and Pillar beyond

Other good family walking/cycling routes start from Ennerdale's Bleach Green parking.

Black Sail makes a superb destination but increased publicity has made it expensive to stay overnight and beds are booked up many months in advance. YHA safeguarding rules dictating that under 12s cannot stay in single sex dorms with a parent have also made it increasingly difficult for families. Skiddaw House (Adventure 40) is a simpler option for families and arguably even more remote.

Bad weather alternative
The full ride would be miserable in bad weather but the lakeside section would be a possibility.

Did you know?

- A mysterious blood-thirsty carnivorous creature named the Girt Dog of Ennerdale killed hundreds of Ennerdale sheep in 1810 before it was hunted down and killed.

- The area is managed by the Forestry Commission and, under the auspices of 'Wild Ennerdale', it is in the initial stages of a long 're-wilding' process, where the extensive conifer plantations are being gradually replaced with native trees.

Adventure 20
Scafell Pike – An Adventurer's Way

Climbing England's highest mountain by the challenging Corridor Route

Start/finish	Seathwaite (Borrowdale) roadside parking (NY 235 122).
Distance	16km (9.9 miles) with 1020m ascent.
Suitable for	● ● ● **Black**. Although one of the hardest undertakings in this book, in good weather this route is a realistic proposition for children – sometimes even those at surprisingly young ages – who are used to doing regular big hikes up mountains. A green option is walking to the photogenic Stockley Bridge from Seathwaite. A blue option is climbing to Styhead Tarn.
Amenities	Toilets at start of route. Refreshments at Seatoller and Rosthwaite.
Public transport	Bus 77/78 from Keswick to Seatoller.
Considerations	This is a big outing, so bring plenty of food and water. The Corridor Route involves a 15m step of grade 1 scrambling (see photo in first part of Introduction). Parents should be able to protect children with ease on this section. The route involves scree and boulder terrain.

To stand on the highest point of a country always has a quirky appeal, and many children will be drawn to the challenge of being able to declare 'I am the highest person in England'. The easiest and most popular route up Scafell Pike is from Wasdale Head via Hollow Stones; it accounts for the vast majority of total ascents of the mountain despite not being an especially good hike. It is nearly always very busy, but on summer weekends it is atrociously so and best avoided unless noisy circuses are your thing. The route we describe here might be a fair bit harder, but it is also considerably better and much more adventurous. It should allow the romance of the mountain to be experienced in a way rarely possible on the quickest route. As such, it is worth waiting for your children to be old enough and strong enough to tackle this route in order to get the most out of England's highest peak.

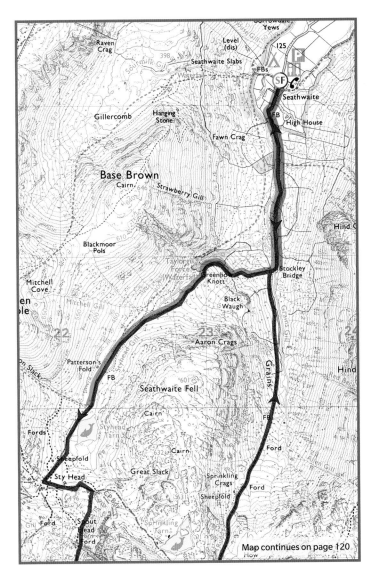

Map continues on page 120

From **Seathwaite**, head through the farm at the road's end and follow the bridleway to the picturesque stone arch of **Stockley Bridge**. Cross the bridge and go through a gate. Ignore the path on the left coming down the valley from Great End. Instead, leave **Grains Gill** behind and head steeply uphill over **Greenhow Knot**. Continue for 2km to **Styhead Tarn** (a tough challenge and possible destination for younger children). Here there are impressive views back down Borrowdale towards the distant Skiddaw. From the stretcher box at the head of the tarn avoid trying to cut off the corner over boggy ground, and instead head left (east) uphill towards **Sprinkling Tarn** for 300m, then take a clear path on the right, descending slightly at first – the Corridor Route. A highlight of the Corridor Route is a short grade 1 scrambling descent midway along – adults going first should have no problem protecting children who face into the rock. Just before a mini tarn on the right of the path, look out for a well-walked cairned path on the left that leaves the Corridor Route. Follow this,

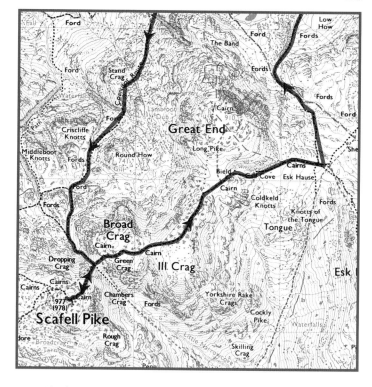

Still going strong near the summit with the crags of Great Gable beyond

joining another path coming up from Piers Gill – the impressively deep arrowhead rift that draws the eye for much of the Corridor Route. A scree-ridden hike will lead to the col between **Broad Crag** and **Scafell Pike**. Turn right here and follow the steep ascent to the highest point in England.

Descent

For tired legs, simply reverse the Corridor route. However, a great adventurous circular hike is possible with only a little extra effort. Return to the col between Scafell Pike and Broad Crag. From here, head upwards to pass the summit of Broad Crag (follow cairns across a substantial boulder field). Dip into another shallow col and take an initially reddish-coloured path roughly north east for 800m – difficult boulder terrain makes this feel longer. Avoid a detour to the summit of Great End and instead descend gradually eastwards on an increasingly easy path towards **Esk Hause**. Then follow a well-walked and well-maintained path that branches off left (northwards) and eventually swings below the impressive northeast face of **Great End** towards Sprinkling Tarn. Directly opposite Great End's large unmistakable central gully, a clear path branches off rightwards. Follow this down Grains Gill to return via Stockley Bridge to Seathwaite.

Scrambling on the Corridor Route with the rift of Piers Gill

Did you know?

- In 1802, the poet Samuel Taylor Coleridge recorded arguably the first rock climb undertaken solely for recreation – a descent of what today is known as Broad Stand, a notoriously dangerous route on the crags of Scafell. During his climb he 'laughed' at himself 'for a madman' but felt the 'fantastic pleasure' of his soul 'swimming through the air as if a flight of starlings in a wind'.

- A spitfire aeroplane crashed killing its pilot, Donald Loudon, on nearby Ill Crag in the winter of 1947.

Bad weather alternative
Save this for good weather. Try a lower level hike.

The Northern Lakes

At the helm near Glencoyne Bay with Silver Crag beyond (Adventure 26)

Adventure 21
Squirrel Nutkin's Island, Derwent Water

Boating out to 'Owl Island' from the Beatrix Potter
story, paddling, swimming and exploring

Start/finish	Keswick area. Limited considerate roadside parking near Calfclose Bay (NY 270 213) or National Trust Great Wood car park 300m further up the road towards Keswick. In Keswick, the main marinas with boat hire are signposted from the town centre.
Distance	1km (0.6 miles) one way on the water from Calfclose Bay; 1.5km (0.9 miles) from Nichol End or slightly further still from Derwent Water Marina.
Suitable for	● Blue. This is ideal for families with enough competent paddlers. Kayaks, canoes, rowing and even sailboats are a common sight on the island. See Appendix C for details of where to hire boats and safety equipment in Keswick.
Amenities	Keswick
Public transport	Keswick is well served by bus
Considerations	Anything more than a breeze will make this trip considerably harder. From the roadside parking, scope out an easy route down to the shore before attempting portage of boats as there are some steep and loose paths in the area.

Imagine a flotilla of tiny rafts carrying red squirrels across to the wooded island in the centre of Derwent Water – that is exactly what Lakeland author Beatrix Potter did in *The Tale of Squirrel Nutkin*. The cheeky protagonist taunts the owl Big Brown on 'Owl Island'. The owl eventually snaps and Nutkin escapes, but only after losing his bushy tail. Owl Island is St Herbert's Island – the largest of the islands where public access is allowed on Derwent Water. Those with their own craft might paddle out from Calfclose Bay on the eastern shore. It is further – but still viable – to make the trip from one of the boat hire locations in Keswick. Derwent Water itself is a magical place to be on the water, with views of Skiddaw to the north, Catbells to the west, the wooded slopes of High Seat to the east and the Borrowdale fells to the south. There is an absolute glut of brilliant trees for climbing on the island and even a few secret dens and bankings which were once reputably a cell – home to the hermit St Herbert himself.

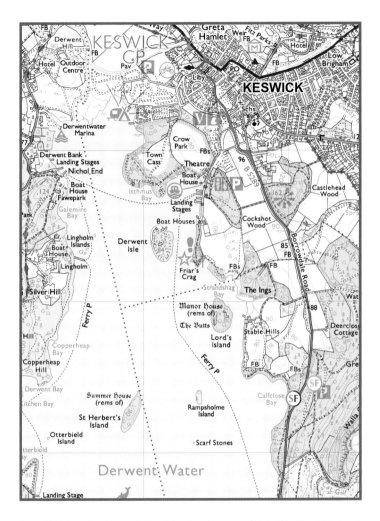

From **Calfclose Bay**, **Rampsholme Island** makes a good first objective. This is not as interesting or large as St Herbert's, but it is useful as it is situated about halfway between St Herbert's and the shore. There are good landing spots all along the east shore of **St Herbert's**. Most boaters arriving from **Keswick** land their craft on the

By the beach at St Herbert's Island with Catbells forming the skyline

island's northern tip. Derwent Water is much narrower at its northern end and starting from Keswick means that you stay closer to the shoreline and get a closer look at the private **Derwent Isle** with its impressive residence.

Bad weather alternative
Make haste to the pencil museum in Keswick.

Did you know?

- Derwent Water, along with Coniston, was used to film 2016's *Swallows and Amazons* and fans of the Walker family's antics will love exploring St Herbert's twisting wooded paths and pebbly beaches.

- Lord's Island, which lies close to the shore north of Calfclose Bay is a protected area for wildlife. The National Trust – the owners – ask that boaters do not land and do not paddle between the island and the shore.

- The mansion on Derwent Isle was built in 1778. It is now owned by the National Trust and visits are allowed a few times per year but private tenants actually live in the house and the whole island is out of bounds to boaters.

Adventure 22
Catbells and Derwent Water

Taking a boat ride to climb a well-loved fell
and paddling in Derwent Water

Start	Keswick. The 'lakeside' car park (NY 265 229) is best for the launch. The route starts from Hawse End landing (NY 252 214) where the Keswick Launch will deposit you.
Finish	The primary route finishes at High Brandelhow landing (NY 253 197) from where you can catch the return Launch to Keswick.
Distance	4.5km (2.8 miles) main route; 3km (1.9 miles) there-and-back option. 6.5km (4 miles) if the Launch is not used or with a round trip from Hawse End. 400m ascent.
Suitable for	● Blue. All ages – the ascent is steep in parts but the fell is a good challenge for 3–6 year olds.
Amenities	Refreshments and public toilets near Keswick lakeshore.
Public transport	Regular ferry from Keswick to Hawse End and back from High Brandelhow. Keswick is well served by buses.
Considerations	The scrambling is not so hard as to rule out taking very young children in backpacks. The full walk may be too long for very young families who may prefer to retrace their steps from the summit.

Catbells is something of a rite of passage for youngsters visiting the Lake District. Its slopes teem with a wide cross section of the general public and it is far from a lonely secret place. That said, the marvellous steep scrambly walk up the fell's shapely north ridge seems to delight young and old alike and would be top of many people's lists of family outings. Children who love scrambling will relish finding numerous hands-on routes on the rockier steps of the crest. The most adventurous approach is taking the launch across Derwent Water – this has the advantage of avoiding the difficulty of parking in the Catbells vicinity. The primary route circles back across the lower hillside to the coves of the lakeshore.

Taking the Keswick launch to Hawse End gives a scenic and enticing approach to Catbells – the fell's distinctive curving form rises straight out of the water. From the landing, a sign points away from the lake to the main **Catbells** path, which starts near a

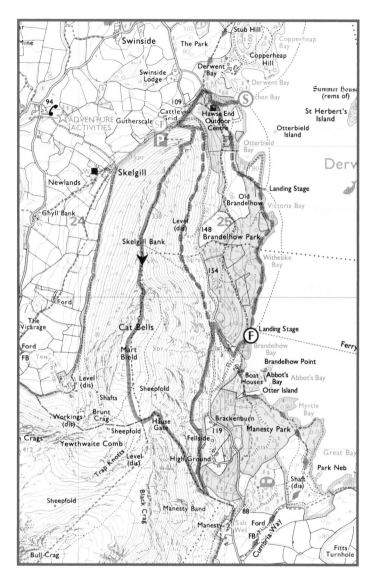

At the summit looking out over Derwent Water

cattle grid (where you will find limited parking). Few directions are necessary – follow the main ridge path up to the summit. The first scrambly section quickly appears before any complaints about the steepness can start. Views of Skiddaw, Keswick and High Seat also entertain. After two mini summit hummocks, the true summit looms impressively ahead and is reached by a longer, easy scrambling section.

If energy permits, continue along the soon grassier ridge. After 700m, at an obvious wide grassy col with a clear junction of paths, turn left and descend the Derwent Water flank of the fell. This path is well built and heads further south for 600m. Take the first opportunity (not the path closed for erosion) to turn left (north). The good path now contours the fellside above the lake for more than 1km until it meets the road. Here, by taking the first leftward rising path the start of the ridge can be regained at the cattle grid. More interestingly, take the path directly across the road which leads down to the lakeshore at **High Brandelhow** landing. Either wait for a launch or continue along the lakeshore path, passing numerous pebbly paddling spots and a sculpture of some large hands called Entrust. At the gate by the next landing, veer left and emerge on a lane at **Hawse End Outdoor Centre**. Turn right here and then right again to Hawse End landing or left on a path from the same point signed to Catbells to your parking space.

Bad weather alternative
Stay on the launch or visit some of Keswick's indoor attractions

Did you know?

- Fans of the Peter Rabbit series of books by Lakeland author Beatrix Potter should be on the look-out for Mrs Tiggy-Winkle's house on this route. The hedgehog washerwoman lived on the slopes of Catbells and the hamlet of Little Town, which can be seen from the summit, was home to Lucie in the story.

- Derwent Water is the home of Britain's rarest fish, the vendace.

- The name Catbells may derive from cat bield meaning 'home of the wild cat' so keep your eyes peeled for feline sightings.

Celebratory scenes after a successful climb of Catbells

Adventure 23
Taking on Whinlatter's Quercus Trail

Technical mountain biking on a purpose-built trail
with optional activities to suit all ages

Start/finish	Braithwaite area. Park at Whinlatter Forest visitor centre car park for a fee (NY 207 245), or there is limited roadside parking available nearby.
Distance	7.5km (4.7 miles); optional shorter 3.5km (2.2 miles) loop.
Suitable for	● ● Black. The Quercus Trail is suited to older children with good fitness, excellent bike handling and competent off-road mountain biking skills – with eight years of age being realistic to consider it. Blue. Two alternative routes on wide tracks for developing bikers. Options for non-cycling activities suitable for all ages.
Amenities	Café and toilets at the visitor centre
Public transport	77 or 77A from Keswick.
Considerations	Trail maps and orienteering maps are available at the visitor centre and shop. For the Quercus Trail, a helmet is essential. There are tree and rock hazards – although drops and exposure are minimal. Geared bikes with well-serviced brakes are a must for its narrow lines, sharp bends and technical terrain, though suspension is not needed – normal sturdy children's bikes will suffice. Parents may find it useful to assess the Quercus route first. Bike hire is available from Cyclewise next to the visitor centre.

The Quercus Trail would have blown our minds when we were young. It is a specially designed entry-level off-road mountain biking trail with just the right degree of technical challenge to make it an enthralling adventure for adults, yet set at such a standard so as to keep it within reach of strong biking children. If this had been available to us and our pals – easily spotted in the mid-80s riding around local woods, wastelands and streets on our colourful single speed BMXs imagining that we had ET on our handlebars – we would have wanted to ride the trail again and again and again...(even if we would have struggled without gears). It is simply amazing and not to be missed. Our advice: if you are not ready for it – get ready for it!

Entry level mountain biking on the Quercus Trail

The Quercus Trail is signed with a blue arrow on a white background and no map is needed. Begin at Cyclewise and follow signs uphill for 80m or so to the starting gate. The route winds gradually down through the trees to reach a forest track onto which you turn left. Follow this for a short distance looking out for the Quercus Trail signed off rightwards down into the trees – this is easily missed. The route now wends brilliantly down through the dense trees and bushes, with a neat bit on some duck boards and stunning sharp bends with great cambers not to be taken too quickly. Wide forest tracks negotiate an area of felled forest. Nearing the road, the route leaves the forest track and winds uphill on a narrower trail to a road crossing. A series of uphill S bends lead to a junction with the short-cut option. Unless you are really exhausted, do not opt for the short cut, but continue the full loop. Having ignored the short-cut, more of the technical S bends – with the odd hummock or two – intercede before the taller forest trees swallow you once more. Here you will feel like Luke Skywalker or Princess Leia flying through the forests of Endor in The Return of the Jedi, for this passage is truly sensational. A stone circle seating area is met before the ascent; it is a good place for a recharge if needed. The climb back up the hill uses a combination of amenably angled wide forest tracks and an impressive series of switchbacks on a narrow trail, with one excellent surprise descent to a wooden bridge. The route continues homewards to the visitor centre – incorporating a tremendously exciting raised gangway and other delights on route.

Blue biking alternatives

Alternative one
Revelin Moss Hiking Trail, 2.25km. Young accompanied bikers have permission to cycle on this. Start from the Revelin Moss car park on the opposite side of the road to the visitor centre. The ride follows the yellow-marked walking trail up Grisedale Gill. A gradual but continuous climb is made on the wide track uphill, until a narrow path is taken on the right. Cross the wooden bridge and see if you can ride the short connecting trail to the next track! At the next track, turn left uphill to a bench at the top of the climb. Continue on the track downhill to the car park.

The Revelin Moss trail is also a green walking and orienteering route.

Alternative two
To Bob's Seat and back, 3.25km. From the visitor centre car park follow the C2C 71 route through a gate. Continue climbing gently round the mountain on the forest track, ignoring the 71 when it branches off downhill on the right. Bob's Seat is a bench. It is eventually reached and allows scenic views of a swathe of hills including Skiddaw, Helvellyn, Catbells and Causey Pike. Return the way you have come, enjoying the freewheeling fruits of your uphill efforts!

Concentrating for the technical boarded section near the end of the Quercus Trail

Maps

We have not included OS mapping for this route. More suitable free mapping can be found online at www.forestry.gov.uk/pdf/Whinlattercyclingmap.pdf or search 'Whinlatter cycling map'. Walking trail maps (including the Revelin Moss route) are at www.forestry.gov.uk/pdf/Whinlatter-walking-trails-map_Sep2011.pdf or search 'Whinlatter walking map'.

Bad weather alternative

Not an unpleasant spot in bad weather, though the Quercus Trail would become appreciably harder. Take shelter in the visitor centre.

Did you know?

- Those who know their Latin will know that *quercus* means 'oak' – one of the many types of tree found on the route

- Whinlatter Forest Park also offers a range of activities including: a 'GO Ape' high-wire tree route with zipwires (paid), orienteering, nature talks, nature trails, walking loops and excellent children's adventure playgrounds.

- Red squirrels are common at Whinlatter and the visitor centre also has a live camera feed of an osprey's nest.

Adventure 24
Castlerigg Stone Circular

Exploring an ancient Druid circle, scrambling or
going rock climbing on Church Crag

Start/finish	Keswick area. There is a small car park and roadside parking at St John's in the Vale hamlet (NY 306 225).
Distance	6.5km (4 miles)
Suitable for	● Blue. This is mainly easy terrain, though often boggy, with one short steep ascent.
Amenities	There's a café at the climbing wall on route, and often an ice cream van near the stone circle.
Public transport	The 73 bus from Keswick to start at the stone circle.
Considerations	A shorter one-way walk of 3km (1.9 miles) can be made, if an adult makes the return journey for the car.

This delightful circuit makes the most of a trip to the superbly positioned Castlerigg Stone Circle. The hilltop environs are magnificent and children will enjoy racing around the 5,000-year-old megaliths with the wind at their heels. The views are superlative all the way around the circuit and there are several scrambling opportunities as well as a visit to the secluded Tewet Tarn. This walk is best started at the hidden-away hamlet of St John's in the Vale, making Castlerigg and an amenable café and adventure playground at Keswick Climbing Wall a halfway point. It is easy to leave tired children with an adult here while other party members complete the circuit. The climbing wall itself is a good wet weather distraction. Better still, staff can organise outdoor family climbing on Church Crag at St John's in the Vale.

Start from the small church and outdoor centre, with a memorial stone and lookout above it to explore. Take the path northwards opposite the church over a stile across boggy pasture, gaining superb views towards Skiddaw and Blencathra. The path skirts right of **Church Crag** (a decent spot to introduce children to rock climbing – see details below).

After 1km, cross a stile and then descend to the lovely **Tewet Tarn**. There are some scrambling possibilities to be sought out on this high plateau and the

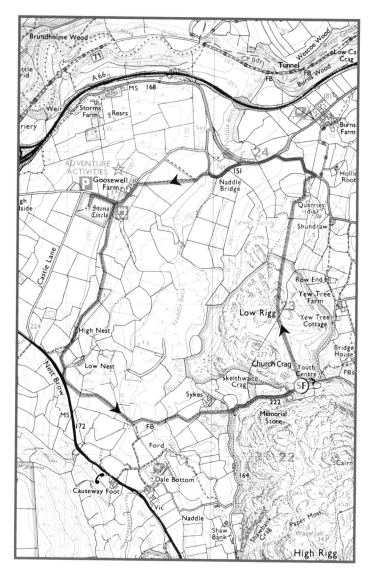

A spring trip to Tewet Tarn with Blencathra's summit dusted in snow

eagle-eyed will spot the stone circle from here. Continue in the same direction, crossing a mini gorge good for exploring and then veer down rightwards to meet a minor road. Turn left here, then left again after 250m and left again shortly afterwards where the road merges. Take a footpath on the bend which leads up to the lane where the stone circle is found. The climbing wall has a café and adventure trail (small fee). Turn left along the lane to reach the **stone circle**, noting a path descending leftwards just before its entrance (our onward route).

Running rings round the hilltop stone circle at Castlerigg

After visiting the stones, rejoin the path near the entrance descending south through fields with views towards the Derwent Fells. At a fork, go left signed to St John's to meet the A591. Turn left, almost immediately taking another path down left with yet more impressive views of the craggy High Rigg ahead. Pass a hollow tree, which is good for hiding in and, after 600m, fork leftwards to St John's. Cross a narrow wooden footbridge and climb slightly to the right of **Sykes Farm**, where there is a series of mini scrambling humps for children right by the path. Where the path meets a track, follow signs steeply uphill back to your starting point.

Learning the ropes at Church Crag near St John's with Blencathra beyond

Bad weather alternative
There is parking close to the stone circle if the weather is too bad to do the whole walk. Try out the indoor climbing wall.

To arrange an outdoor climbing session at Church Crag, contact Keswick Climbing Wall on 01768 772000.

Did you know?

- Castlerigg Stone Circle is a Neolithic monument dating from around 3,000BC. No-one knows why it was built and legend has it that it is impossible to count the stones – you will always get a different number!

Adventure 25
Riding on Keswick's old railway

Traffic free cycling on a disused rail line from Keswick to Threlkeld following the course of the River Greta

Start/finish	Keswick. Park at Keswick leisure centre (fee) near Fitz Park (NY 269 237).
Distance	5km (3.1 miles) there and back to the bridge at the end of Brundholme Wood. 10km (6.2 miles) there and back for the full ride when it reopens
Suitable for	● Blue. There is very little height gain on well-surfaced paths, making it manageable for most families. A green option is to ride just the first section before the A66 underpass.
Amenities	It is possible to end the ride following C2C signage into Fitz Park, where there is a seasonal ice cream van and a café. There are public toilets in the town centre car park. Threlkeld has an excellent tea room and public toilets.
Public transport	Keswick bus station is a hub for northern Lake District routes. Bikes can be hired from Keswick. See Appendix B for details.
Considerations	In 2015, Storm Desmond destroyed two bridges on this ride and severely damaged several more areas. After a huge fundraising effort, a massive rebuilding project is under way, with the intention that the full ride to Threlkeld will reopen in 2020. Check with www.lakedistrict.gov.uk for the latest information and check for updates at www.cicerone.co.uk/956/updates. A very short last section of the full ride is on the village road into Threlkeld and there is a similarly short section on a path beside (not on) the busy A66.

The Keswick to Threlkeld railway ride was, prior to the catastrophic storm damage in 2015, one of the finest traffic-free family cycling routes in the Lake District. It linked the bustling northern Lakes centre of Keswick with the quiet village of Threlkeld, which nestles under the precipitous slopes of Blencathra. However, in 2015 floods decimated the route – two of the crucial bridges spanning the river

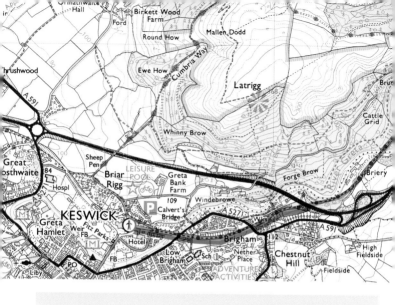

were washed away, up to three more were structurally damaged and a section of riverside path collapsed. At the time of going to print, the ride was still only feasible up to the bridge at the end of Brundholme Wood making an enjoyable but frustrating 5km there-and-back route. The ride follows the course of the River Greta through an unlikely gorge and, before the storms, it was part of the popular C2C long-distance route. As the original route should reopen again in 2020, a full route description is given. A highlight is the vertiginous duck boards, which cling to the side of the Greta's gorge high above the river before Briery. The River Greta is fast flowing, particularly near Keswick, and paddling is not advised on the stretch of the ride currently open. There are some suitable dappled paddling spots nearer the source of the river. These can be reached on foot by following the route as far as permissible from the Threlkeld end.

The route leaves directly from the car park, which is beside the old station platform. Follow the course of the former railway on good gravelly surfaces through the outskirts of Keswick. Cross the first of many bridges over both the river and a road and, as the houses are left behind, begin to climb very gradually to rise above the river and pass under the yawning concrete bridge of the A66. Shortly afterwards, the route curves around the gorge side and leaves the railway course temporarily on a purpose-built, wooden, slatted gangway, which twists and turns and clings to the side of the slope high above the river. It is immense fun to ride on but may in future years be

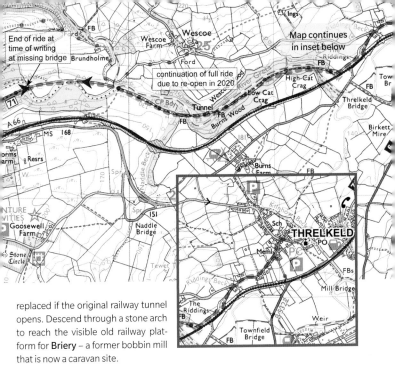

replaced if the original railway tunnel opens. Descend through a stone arch to reach the visible old railway platform for **Briery** – a former bobbin mill that is now a caravan site.

The Lake District was the bobbin capital of the world in the mid 19th century. Briery bobbin mill made bobbins for the silks in Queen Elizabeth II's wedding gown and for the wire woven into old pound notes.

After the caravan site, cross twin bridges over a bend in the river where the eroded gorge is impressively on view. After a further 900m at a lower elevation through woods, the first missing bridge at the eastern end of **Brundholme Wood** is reached. At the time of writing, the ride stopped here, where there is access to a large pebble beach.

Extended route (expected to reopen in 2020)

Cross the bridge and continue on a more open riverside section with views of the high fells before re-crossing the river several times and joining a section of track through a stone cutting and a short **tunnel**. The path eventually emerges through a gate onto a segregated path beside the busy A66. This is followed for 200m and then veers leftwards still on a pavement path on the minor road into **Threlkeld** with

Bridge Over The River Greta

up close views of Blencathra's dramatic ridges. The final 100m or so to the toilets and café is on the very minor village road, and will be manageable for most families.

Return by the same route.

Bad weather alternative
This is not an unreasonable wet weather ride. There are plenty of indoor diversions in Keswick (refer to Appendix E).

Did you know?

- The River Greta, at 11km long, is one of the shortest rivers in the UK. It boasts diverse wildlife such as otters, trout, salmon, eels, wrens and dippers.

- Greta Hall in Keswick was the home of the poet Robert Southey, poet laureate from 1813–43. He wrote the first published version of the *Goldilocks and the Three Bears* story – although the original consumer of the bears' porridge was not the blonde-haired little girl, but a little old vagrant woman!

Adventure 26
Ullswater's four island challenge

Boating, paddling and exploring the islands

Start/finish	Glenridding area. Park for a fee at the National Trust car park at Glencoyne Bridge (NY 388 188). Those without boats or transport should start from Glenridding.
Distance	4km (2.5 miles) over water in total to visit all four islands from Glencoyne, and slightly less from Glenridding (red). Cherry Holm Island from Glenridding is a 400m round trip (green). Norfolk Island from Glencoyne is a 1km (0.6 miles) round trip and is blue.
Suitable for	●●● Red. The full route is the hardest water-based outing in this book. Good equipment is essential. A one-to-one adult to child ratio is needed for younger families and parents will need good boat-handling skills in order to reach more than just Cherry Holm. Easier blue and green options as above.
Amenities	Glenridding
Public transport	Bus 508 from Windermere or 208 from Keswick.
Considerations	A variety of boats can be hired at Glenridding from Glenridding Sailing Centre or St Patrick's Boat Landing. Those with their own craft will prefer to launch from the quieter shores at Glencoyne and should take care crossing the road from the car park to the lakeshore. Care must also be taken when mooring. Avoid windy or unsettled weather conditions.

The Lake District's second biggest lake is encircled by high craggy fells at its southern foot. Here, Ullswater narrows and the Patterdale road skirts close to the shoreline, providing glimpses of numerous tempting pebble beaches and inviting launching spots. A cursory examination of the water reveals a number of enticing islands. It is possible to visit four of them by kayak or canoe, though a round trip alighting at all four is quite an expedition and should be saved for a calm day. Hiring boats at Glenridding allows a good shorter adventure to just one island – particularly suitable for novice adult rowers. Children of all ages will enjoy taking the helm and finding the best places to dock. Taking a picnic to have on your own island while waving at the passengers on the Ullswater steamers adds to the fun.

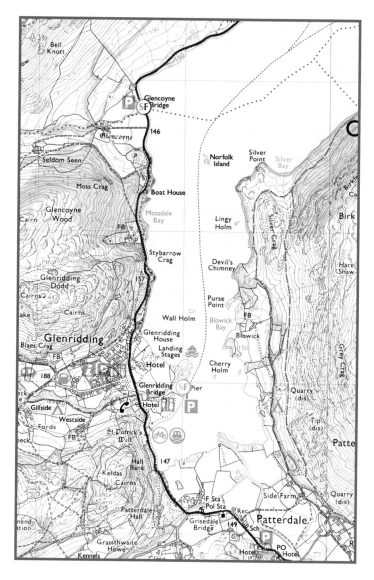

If launching from Glencoyne, head out to explore Norfolk Island first and then decide whether to continue. From Glenridding, Cherry Holm is the logical first port of call.

Norfolk Island is the most northerly, largest and rockiest of the group. It is an exciting place for children to explore, though keep a close eye on them as there are some fairly high drops. Norfolk boasts a shady harbour on the western side, a little rocky bluff to scramble up, seasonal blackberries to pick and a variety of paths. It is grassy and shelter can always be found there, making it the ideal picnicking spot.

From here, the tiny **Lingy Holm** beckons 400m to the south and closer to Ullswater's eastern shore where it rises to **Silver Crag**. Take care mooring here as the rocks can be slippery.

It is at least 600m south-east to get to **Wall Holm** – a heather-topped island blighted somewhat by the poo of the numerous geese that congregate thereabouts. Again, this island has a lovely natural harbour.

Exploring Wall Holm on Ullswater

Waving at the Ullswater steamer from Norfolk Island

The final island is **Cherry Holm**. This is the simplest and nearest to reach from Glenridding. It has its own pebbly beach and a well-climbed old oak tree to look out from. Mooring is simple and there are grassy spots for picnics.

Bad weather alternative
Take a trip on the Ullswater steamer or visit Aira Force (see route 27).

Did you know?

- Ullswater was the site of the first 200mph+ water speed record, set by Donald Campbell's Bluebird K7 in July 1955.

- In the 1950s and 1960s Sir Donald Campbell, who followed in the footsteps of his speed demon father Sir Malcolm Campbell, set eight world water and land speed records. Four of these were set on Lake Coniston. However, after one run too many, he tragically lost his life on Coniston when his Bluebird K7 took flight.

On the stone bridge right above the main fall, Aira Force

The thundering cascade of Aira Force

Adventure 27
The cascades of Aira Force

Visiting waterfalls, stream paddling, island hopping and tree climbing

Start/finish	Ullswater. Park at Park Brow National Trust car park on the A5091 (NY 397 205). Alternatively, the route can also be accessed from the main Aira Force NT parking on the A592 or the High Cascade NT car park on A5091.
Distance	2.5km (1.6 miles), with a shorter 2km (1.2 miles) variation.
Suitable for	🟢 Green.
Amenities	Café and toilets in the main Aira Force car park
Public transport	508 from Windermere or Penrith. Ullswater Steamer from Glenridding or Pooley Bridge.
Considerations	Paths are well-maintained, but cliff edges require considerable caution – especially if you stray from the paths. Paddling and scrambling locations are well away from the main falls. They require careful assessment, close supervision and should be avoided after heavy rain

Perennially popular, but no less delightful, this outing involves an encounter with one of England's most impressive and historic waterfalls. Aira Force has proved alluring since the Romantic period when 18th century visitors in search of the sublime would potter through the woods to marvel at the power of nature as expressed by a 20m plunging waterfall chasing and dashing its way down a dark wooded ravine. Young adventurers will follow in their footsteps – finding much to entertain them on a trail punctuated by tremendous opportunities for paddling, island hopping, climbing trees and scurrying around the dry and easy-angled polished slabs near the High Cascade.

Follow the path downhill from Park Brow car park through two gates to a crooked signpost. Trend left then back right to descend steep steps gaining superb views of the impressive **Aira Force**. Cross the bridge below the falls, then after a few metres branch off left up steps to reach the bridge above the main falls – have a look at this, but do not cross the river. Instead, continue upstream on the right-hand (eastern) bank

The daffodils on the shores of Ullswater inspired William Wordsworth's most famous poem.

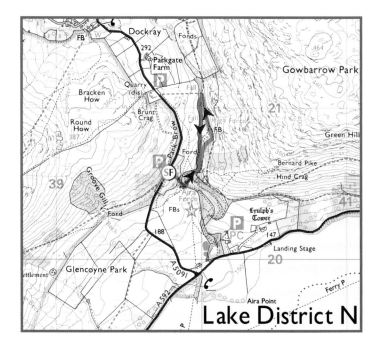

– dependent on water levels, good paddling and island hopping opportunities mate-
rialise on the level section after 50m. After another 150m, a path leads down to a
wooden bridge above a pool at a narrow gorge with more falls (marked as High Force
on the map). It is an optional shortcut to connect with the path on the other bank.
Continue upstream passing another level section with some fun wooded islands and
other pleasant paddling areas until reaching the bridge at the higher cascade with a
series of easy-angled slabs beside small waterfalls. (The path from the High Cascade
car park joins here.) Cross the bridge and follow the path on the right (west) bank
downstream until the approach route is met above Aira Force.

Note: If parking at the lower car park off the A592, head uphill from the car park
but stay on the left (west) bank so that the waterfall is encountered by the dramatic
descent down the steps, where the main route is joined. To return to the lower car
park use the left (east) bank in descent, crossing over the river at the plantation.

The pebble beach by Ullswater Pier is easily reached by following signs from the
café or lower car park for 100m.

Adventure 28
Galleny Force and Smithymire Island

Paddling, swimming at the Fairy Glen, walking,
tree climbing and swinging

Start/finish	Borrowdale. Park at Stonethwaite (NY 263 137). There is usually a space on the roadside well before the village.
Distance	3.5km (2.2 miles)
Suitable for	🟢 Green. Flattish but on rough paths.
Amenities	There's a cosy tea room and a pub in Stonethwaite and a child-friendly cafe by Shepherd's Crag a couple of miles north on the Borrowdale road.
Considerations	The water activities are described in summer low water conditions. After heavy rain, Galleny Force becomes a raging torrent and is dangerous. All children will need close supervision in moving water. The rock slabs beside the water can be slippery. Take water shoes, wetsuits and goggles to make the most of the clear waters.

This scenic section of Stonethwaite Beck is a paddler's paradise for all ages with safe shallows and deeper pools for swimmers. The 'Fairy Glen' around the cascades of Galleny Force and Smithymire Island has been frequented by bathers for generations. Smithymire Island is surrounded mainly by low and slow flowing water and it only just merits the name of 'island'. The pools by the small cascades of Galleny Force just downstream provide a wonderful long swimming channel. On a summer's day, cooling off in the crystalline waters encircled by the craggy Borrowdale Fells is a sure-fire way to relax. Children will not sit still here, for there are abundant rocky stretches, mini channels and water-worn slabs to explore. The walk into Fairy Glen is a delight in itself at any time of year.

From Stonethwaite, continue along the dead-end road then cut left on a path through the extensive riverside campsite. The path continues, reaching an **island** in the river after 800m where there are usually rope swings. Cross a small footbridge and in 300m, the pools of **Galleny Force** are reached just after a gate. There is great paddling in all but the highest water conditions. A 5m wide channel of water gouged between small cliff walls creates a trough deep enough to swim down for 30m in its centre. The latter is not suitable for small children and adults need to check depth and exit points prior to children getting in. Above the channel there are two small cascades.

A little further upstream are the lovely paddling areas around **Smithymire Island** and a second smaller swimming channel. Upstream of this is an area of wider slabby rock, good for scrambling in dry, low water conditions.

Smithymire Island is formed by the confluence of Langstrath Beck, Greenup Gill and another very small tributary. There are a few ways onto the island and it makes a great place to explore.

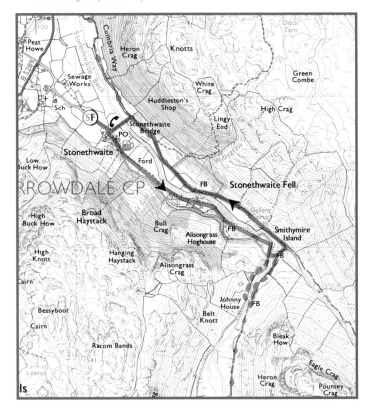

It's warmer than you think – in the long channel at Galleny Force

For a round trip, continue on the riverside path 300m above the island to cross a footbridge and return by a path on the opposite bank to another small bridge at Smithymire Island. Turn left at a gate and use the bridleway to return towards **Stonethwaite**. Pass a yew tree that is good for climbing before eventually crossing a bridge on the left to reach the village after 1.4km.

Bad weather alternative
This route can still be enjoyed on a miserable day, or in colder weather, when children can paddle in their wellies.

Did you know?

- The best swimming area is the 30m-long channel downstream of Galleny Force. In low water, it is even possible to duck behind the main waterfall to sit on a hidden rock seat.

Adventure 29
Buttermere bothying – Dubs Hut and Warnscale Head

Hiking to high mountain bothies and possibly
staying overnight, visiting waterfalls

Start/finish	Honister Pass (NY 225 136) or Gatesgarth Farm at the eastern end of Buttermere (NY 196 150). You need to pay for parking at Honister Pass (enquire in the shop about leaving cars overnight), or there's roadside parking above Gatesgarth Farm.
Distance	Dubs Hut is just over 2km (1.2 miles) from Honister Hause or 3km (1.9 miles) from Gatesgarth Farm. Warnscale is 2.5km (1.6 miles) from both.
Suitable for	● ● Blue. A simple walk in from Honister to Dubs with only 130m ascent. Red with 430m ascent from Gatesgarth Farm.
Amenities	Cafés and toilets at Buttermere and Honister.
Public transport	77 bus from Keswick to Honister.
Considerations	Warnscale is located in very precipitous terrain – only visit in good visibility and be aware that children will need close supervision outside it. Dubs is on far flatter ground. Check bothy status at www.mountainbothies.org.uk before setting out. Refer to the section on bothying in the introduction for general information and code of conduct. As there are two bothies in close proximity, there is a good chance that one will be empty but if there is no space, be prepared to make the return trip. Both bothies are very basic with no toilet facilities. Both have nearby water sources. Warnscale has sleeping platforms for four people, and Dubs has no platforms at all but is a bigger space.

Both Dubs Hut and Warnscale Head bothies sit in majestic surroundings, cradled between the dramatic fin of Fleetwith Pike and the craggy head of Haystacks high above Buttermere. Both used to be old quarry huts. Getting to the bothies is an exciting outing whether you go to explore and perhaps make a hot drink inside, or whether you pack your gear on your back to spend the night at one of the two. Despite their altitude, the bothies can be reached without a mammoth effort thanks to the high road at Honister Pass, from where a disused quarry tramway leads easily to Dubs Hut at the former Dubs Quarry. A more strenuous yet rewarding approach can also be made from Buttermere directly up the side of Warnscale Beck. The bothies are spartan and have few facilities, though both have fireplaces (bring fuel). Warnscale Head bothy can be tricky to locate.

From **Honister Pass**, take the track leaving the parking area uphill in the direction of Buttermere. This is well used, particularly by visitors to the paid via ferrata at the mines. After about 150m look out for a path splitting off left from the main track. Take this up the hillside – it soon becomes the obvious straight line course of a disused tramway which leads directly in less than 2km to **Dubs Hut** (NY 209 134). To continue to visit Warnscale Head bothy (NY 205 133) is red. Descend south to ford **Warnscale Beck** at a plank or stepping stones and continue uphill towards the rocky hump of **Little Round How**. Look out for a small path leaving the main one rightwards after

At Dubs Hut looking towards the Buttermere Fells

200m which winds down the hillside crossing a minor tributary to reach a small cove where the tiny **bothy** hides from view – it is surprisingly hard to locate and do not attempt to do so in the dark or less than perfect visibility.

Retrace your steps to Dubs Hut. Take the quarry track going east above the dismantled tramline. Bear right at a junction of tracks, passing **Hooper Quarry** and **Bell Crags** then descending to meet the outbound route near Honister.

From **Buttermere**, Warnscale Head bothy is easier to find (though still difficult). Starting from **Gatesgarth Farm**, hike up the road towards Honister for 100m then take the first bridleway on the right, which traverses the hillside. Ignore a path splitting off leftwards after 50m that ascends Fleetwith Edge. Continue on the left-hand

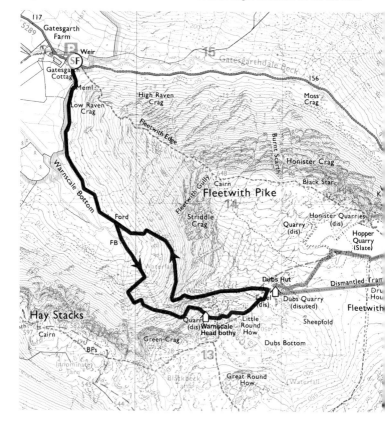

Getting to grips with bothying inside Warnscale Head hut

side of Warnscale Beck. At a fork in the path after 1.2km by a tributary bear right to cross a bridge over **Warnscale Beck** and continue, initially south east, uphill. The path veers rightwards then back left. After an eastwards ramp, cross a stream to a clear path (ignore scree and heather paths leading up right here). Continue for a further 200m or so to where a path leads rightwards over level ground to reach Warnscale Head bothy after 50m. Go further uphill on the main path and then left to reach **Dubs Hut** from here.

From Dubs Hut, it is possible to return to Buttermere by taking a path on the northern side of Warnscale Beck. The path swings around the steep slopes beneath **Striddle Crag** and descends to join the outbound route at the fork in the path.

Warnscale Head bothy can be hard to spot

For those who do stay overnight, the bothies make good staging points for strenuous hikes to Fleetwith Pike or Haystacks summits with older children (red). Little Round How has scrambling potential for older children.

Bad weather alternative

This is not a place to go in bad weather. Take a tour where it's drier underground at Honister slate mine.

Did you know?

- Honister claims to be the last working slate mine (rather than quarry) in the UK. The Westmoreland Green Slate mined here is 450 million years old. Honister slate has been used on the roof of Buckingham Palace.

Adventure 30
The Bowder Stone and King's How

Climbing a mammoth-sized rock and a fell, paddling in the River Derwent

Start/finish	Borrowdale. Bowder Stone National Trust car park (NY 253 167) on the B5289.
Distance	5.6km (3.2 miles) with 320m ascent on the full blue route.
Suitable for	⚫ ⚫ Blue. The terrain is rough and steep and this is a step up from the very easiest fells. Navigation skills and good visibility are required. The green and bad weather alternative to the Bpwder stone is 1km there and back just to the Bowder Stone.
Amenities	Cafés in nearby Grange and Rosthwaite. Toilets at Rosthwaite.
Considerations	Children must be closely supervised at the Bowder Stone. The rock is incredibly slippery in wet conditions. Paddling near Eelstep Brow should only be considered in dry, low water conditions.

The Bowder Stone is one of Lakeland's historical curiosities. One explanation of how the massive boulder came to rest in Borrowdale is that it toppled off the top of King's How more than 10,000 years ago, though others believe it was carried down from Scotland on an Ice Age glacier. The strangely balanced rock is estimated to weigh 2,000 tons and climbing the ladder steps to the top is an absolute must for children, as is shaking hands through a tiny hole under the precariously balanced stone. Towering above the Bowder Stone, the enchanting natural woodlands and slopes of Grange Fell make a superb extended outing for families who are confident at route-finding.King's How is the most visited of the Grange Fell tops and is an excellent place for children to begin making the step up from the very steady paths of Sale Fell or Latrigg to trickier ground. Scrambling onto a large picnic rock on the way up and at the rocky summit gives a taste of more massive things to come when the Bowder Stone is reached on the way back.

From the upper car park, take a path through a gate in the back left hand corner heading north in the opposite direction to the Bowder Stone (there is a distinctive large square boulder in 50m). After 200m, this joins another path near a **cave**. This was fenced off and dangerous at the time of writing due to a landslip on its right side. The path continues to climb gradually, past a scrambling stop at the huge 'picnic' boulder where the looming cliffs of Great End Crag rise beyond. The path swings right, ascending to cross a wall. About 100m later stay on the main path (the right hand fork) just before a second wall. The terrain quickly steepens to climb a well-made rock-stepped path through fantastic birch woodland. About halfway up, a massive horizontal branch reaches up to the path and begs to be climbed. When the gradient eases at a col, the path snakes around right, eventually twisting back left above the crags to the lovely summit of **King's How** and its superb views of Derwent Water and Borrowdale.

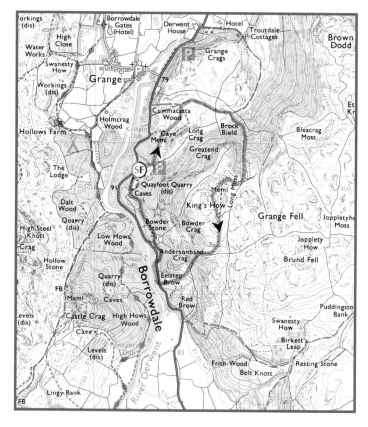

On top of the mighty Bowder Stone

Take the path south off the summit (the opposite direction to your approach). Follow the most well walked option, weaving around the knobbly summit plateau before descending south to reach a T-junction of walls in 400m. Ignore an enticing looking gap which a path appears to go through and take the path to its right following one wall steeply downhill on its right hand side. This crosses a broken wall and leads to the Borrowdale road at a stile (do not be tempted by left trending paths leading to the road further away from the Bowder Stone). Cross the road and take the path beside the **River Derwent** for less than 200m (paddling and skimming spots). Look out for the first exit back onto the road. Re-cross this and follow the signed rocky bridleway opposite, which leads shortly to the **Bowder Stone** in another 200m.

The Bowder Stone has steps to the trough on its rocky top. Children need to be closely supervised here. There is also a scrambling route for older children up the rock's gentler northern end. The stone is incredibly slippery in damp conditions.

Continue for 400m along the track back to the car park.

Tarzan, Lord of King's How

Bad weather green alternative

King's How is not a sensible wet weather summit as the Grange Fell plateau can be dis-orientating in bad weather. Visit the Bowder Stone on its own – even very young children will manage the short walk there and back along the track from the parking area.

Did you know?

- The Bowder Stone is balanced on such an amazingly tiny part of its mass that it is possible to squirm underneath opposite sides of the 2,000 tonne rock to shake hands through a hole in the volcanic rock.

- Kings How is named after King Edward VII, our present queen's great-grandfather. A commemorative plaque can be found near the summit.

Reaching out to shake hands under the Bowder Stone

Adventure 31
Jopplety How and Watendlath

Hiking to a hidden hamlet and tarn, scrambling on fell-top turrets, paddling

Start/finish	Borrowdale. National Trust car park (fee) at Rosthwaite (NY 258 148).
Distance	Full route 7km (4.3 miles) with 350m ascent; shorter option 3km (1.9 miles) with 160m ascent.
Suitable for	⬤ ⬤ Full route blue; shorter option green. All families.
Amenities	Watendlath and Rosthwaite both have cafés and public toilets.
Public transport	Bus 77 or 78 to Rosthwaite from Keswick.
Considerations	The bouldery summits of Jopplety How and Brund Fell have some significant drops and are slippery in damp weather. Children should be closely supervised when scrambling.

The high-up hidden hamlet of Watendlath and its tucked-away tarn have long been popular destinations for hikers. It is a good climb up from Rosthwaite in Borrowdale to reach Watendlath and much excitement can be added with only a little more effort by returning over the castellated turrets of Jopplety How and Brund Fell (415m) – themselves constituent parts of the larger Grange Fell. Here, there are rocky ramparts for young monarchs to guard and scramble on. It is a wild and captivating place to explore and can feel extremely disorientating in less-than-perfect conditions. It is possible to do just the much shorter there-and-back climb up Jopplety How by parking in Watendlath, but this means negotiating the three-mile, single track road to get there – it is not much fun on sunny afternoons!

From Rosthwaite car park, walk back to the main Borrowdale road past the toilets. Turn left across this road and then immediately right by the bus stop on a track signed to Watendlath. Cross a humped stone bridge over Stonethwaite Beck and immediately turn left then right on a hedged path again following signage to Watendlath. Continue through a stony trough uphill to reach a gate into more open hillside and another gate after 200m at a T-junction. Go left to Watendlath. The well-made, stony

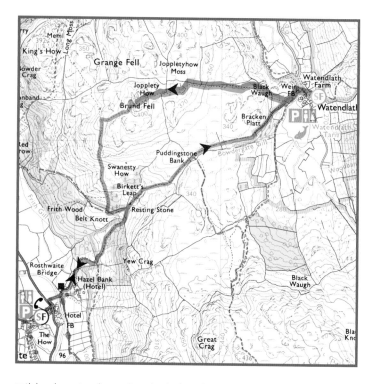

path heads up steeply crossing a beck where the gradient eases for a short time and then steepens again beside a wood to reach a kind of pass after 500m. Views emerge of High Seat and High Tove fells above Watendlath. The good path follows the course of **Bowdergate Gill** gently down the side of a wood to **Watendlath Tarn**. Go left to cross a lovely stone bridge into the **hamlet**.

There are great paddling spots by Watendlath's bridge and tarn beaches.

To return via Jopplety How, cross the stone footbridge and take a faint path leaving rightwards 20m after the wall. This becomes more obvious as it rises through bracken with a short, easy scrambly section. The towers of Jopplety How (nearer to you) on the right and Brund Fell further left are obvious and the route follows the course of the wall up to them. The upper section can be boggy after wet weather. The amount of rock on display will whet any young scrambler's appetite and there is something here for children of all ages. The first triangular face of rock (viewed from the Watendlath approach) has possibilities up the middle and edges for scramblers who are carefully watched and, if necessary, supported from below. A domed hump below it could also be climbed but a buttress further left is probably too steep except for its right end. The path now veers leftwards to a stile in the corner of a doglegged wall. The main path heads straight to the higher Brund Fell turret but a small path rightwards accesses the steep crown of **Jopplety How**.

To reach Jopplety How summit is a slightly exposed scramble with some loose rock but not as forbidding as it first appears. The best line is probably from the col furthest from the wall running down to Watendlath.

The summit rocks of Jopplety How

Ready for a game of pooh sticks at Watendlath Bridge

At the winter's end – following the wall down from Jopplety How to Watendlath

The impressive summit of **Brund Fell**, 100m further along the path, is very easily attained. Perhaps the best scrambling is found on the boulder to the left of the path near the summit, where there is a tiny cave at its top.

The less airy summit of Brund Fell is a great place to admire views of the Derwent valley flanked by Catbells and Skiddaw to the north and Glaramara and the cliffs of Great End to the south.

Continue in the same direction (south-west) picking a way through the numerous tantalising outcrops of the summit plateau to the brow of the hill where Rosthwaite, Castle Crag and the Crook of the **River Derwent** all appear laid out beneath you. The path bears south and traverses the hillside reaching a wood about 1km from the summit. At the bottom of the wood, cross a stile and then turn left slightly uphill for 100m to a gate where turning right regains the outbound route.

Green option
From Watendlath, follow the main route to **Jopplety How** and **Brund Fell** and return by the same route.

Bad weather alternative
Grange Fell's summit plateau is incredibly disorientating in bad weather. Potter about in Rosthwaite or Watendlath.

Adventure 32
Castle Crag and the Cave Hotel

Exploring once inhabited caves, climbing a steep
fell, scrambling, paddling and swinging

Start/finish	Borrowdale. There's a small car park at Grange (NY 253 174) and more parking 200m up the Borrowdale road to Keswick.
Distance	6km (3.7 miles) with 260m ascent
Suitable for	● ● Blue. Tricky terrain for young children. There's a green 3.5km option just visiting the cave.
Amenities	Grange has two tea rooms.
Public transport	Bus 77/78 from Keswick.
Considerations	Cliffs and very steep wooded slopes border much of the summit plateau, so children need to be closely supervised.

Imagine being an explorer living in a cave on a hillside. This route includes visiting two caves used by the mountain adventurer Millican Dalton as a home for nearly 50 years. The larger and higher cave has an upstairs and downstairs level and is known as The Attic. Above it rises the lofty turret of Castle Crag, one of the most interesting mini-summits in the Lake District. Despite its diminutive altitude of 290m, the fell is steep and a surprisingly challenging climb. Getting to the craggy perch of the summit via surreal slate shards of the quarried area justly warrants the coronation of kings and queens of the castle.

Take the track south out of the village towards Rosthwaite. Stay on the lower left-hand fork past the campsites. This area has some great pebble beaches beside the **River Derwent**, which are popular in good weather with picnickers and boaters, although in wet weather, the river quickly rises and becomes dangerously fast-flowing. The path crosses two small footbridges (you may wonder why they are there if you visit in a dry period) and then leaves the river. There are sometimes fun rope swings over the river on the trees in this area. The path climbs slightly away from the river then, 200m after a wall running up the hillside, there is a clear junction. Turn right here uphill fairly steeply to soon reach the two **quarry caves**. The higher cave is

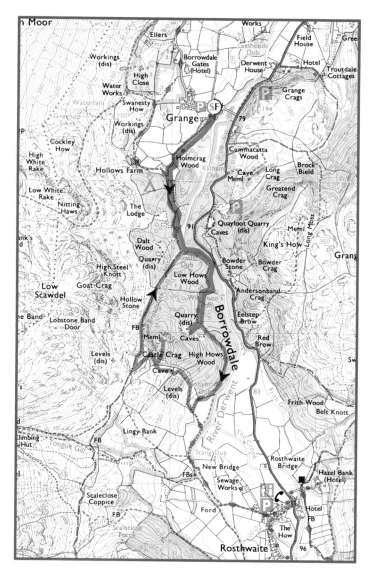

A natural slide at the top of Castle Crag

the more amenable for eating sandwiches and indeed provides a great wet weather picnic destination.

Warning: Do not be tempted to follow the well-walked path in the woods above the uppermost cave. It appears to offer another way to the top, but does not. Neither does it connect with the bridleway along Broadslack Gill. Instead, it leads to dangerous cliffs and a dead end.

From the caves, return to the main path down the hill (the Cumbria Way) and follow this upstream to a gate. Here ignore a path turning right into the woods just before the gate – this heads very steeply to the top on loose scree that is not suitable for children and not much fun for adults. Instead, go through the gate and continue on the track across the clearing for 100m until a very clear path ascends to the right. This is well-maintained and has some stone steps. Follow it uphill, passing through a gate and over a ladder stile on a shoulder below the summit slope. The path then snakes up through the steep grey-blue screes to reach the lofty perch of **Castle Crag** – one of the finest low altitude tops in the region. It has a surreal quarried area where many large shards of slate have been placed upright. Above this, be aware of steep

Descending Broadslack Gill with Skiddaw beyond

drops. The summit has flat picnicking areas, expansive views and a memorial. A slab also offers a natural slide.

From the summit, retrace your steps off the screes but instead of going back over the ladder stile, turn right on a path snaking to meet a bigger bridleway running down **Broadslack Gill**. Turn right and follow this with views of Skiddaw ahead for 1km to reach the outbound route beside the River Derwent. Turn left to return to **Grange**.

Bad weather alternative

The caves are good to visit on a persistently rainy day as they provide good respite from the elements.

Did you know?

- Millican Dalton, the self-styled Professor of Adventure, gave up his job as an insurance clerk to live a spartan existence in what he called 'The Cave Hotel'. He left an inscription in the cave in the early 20th century which reads: Don't Waste Words, Jump to Conclusions.

- The memorial on the summit is to John Hamer and his fellow men of Borrowdale who died in World War 1. The Hamer family gave this land to the National Trust.

Exploring the 'The Cave Hotel'

Adventure 33
Buttermere and Scale Force

Circumnavigating one of Lakeland's famous beauty spots or visiting Lakeland's highest waterfall, paddling, swimming and geocaching

Start/finish	Buttermere. There's a village car park (NY 173 169) and a National Trust car park 200m outside the village towards Crummock Water (NY 174 172).
Distance	7.5km (4.7 miles) from Buttermere. Starting from Gatesgarth and taking the permissive lakeshore path to avoid Buttermere village shortens this by just under 1km. The Scale Force option is 5.5km (3.4 miles).
Suitable for	● Blue. An achievable objective for many walkers, given plenty of time.
Amenities	Toilets and cafés in Buttermere. Syke Farm sells ice cream made on site.
Public transport	Bus 77 from Keswick
Considerations	Bring swimming gear and towels.

The Buttermere circuit is a well-loved family classic – it may not feel as adventurous as many routes in this book, but there is plenty of scope for exploring the alluring gills that feed the lake, a spooky tunnel, fallen trees for balancing acts and dozens of beaches for paddling and stone skimming. There is a relatively easy lakeshore path, a convenient homemade ice cream stop and views of the dramatic craggy fells encircling the lake. It can get exceedingly popular on fine summer days, but even at peak times there are so many small beaches that you can be sure to find one to yourselves. Those seeking a less well-travelled path should head for Scale Force; at 52m it is the highest dropping waterfall in the Lake District and after wet weather it makes a dramatic goal. This alternative route has a more adventurous feel with trickier and sometimes boggy terrain.

The walk around Buttermere needs very little explanation. The direction can easily be changed and it is equally enjoyable to start from the parking at Gatesgarth. From **Buttermere** village, follow the bridleway down the left side of the Fish Inn. After about 200m there is a raised up carved log for children to practise balancing

along. Here, the path splits – the right-hand gated option goes to Scale Force (see alternative route, below). Take the main bridleway signed to the lake to reach the shore in 500m at **Sourmilk Gill**. In bone dry conditions the initial waterworn slabs of the gill can provide fun scrambling. Turn left and follow the well-surfaced lakeside path through **Burtness Wood** for 1.5km. On this stretch there are further fallen trees set up for balancing and often dens to hide in or build in the woods. Cross a small bridge over **Comb Beck**, where there are boulder hopping, paddling and scrambling opportunities. In 1km the path crosses **Peggy's Bridge** at the head of the lake under the looming fin of Fleetwith Pike to emerge after 500m at **Gatesgarth Farm** (there is often an ice-cream van here). Turn left along the road for 200m then take the rockier roadside and then lakeside path passing numerous pebbly beaches. After 1.5km there are a few very easy, scrambly steps followed by a dark and echoey interlude in **Hassness Tunnel**. At the end of the lake, take the right-hand bridleway option to regain **Buttermere village**.

> The 30m Hassness Tunnel is a historical curiosity. Supposedly the 19th century landowner made his labourers painstakingly cut it out of the rock to keep them from being idle in the winter months.

Scale Force alternative

Where the Buttermere village bridleway splits, take the right-hand gated option signed to Scale Force. Follow this over the stone **Scale Bridge** (a good hiding place

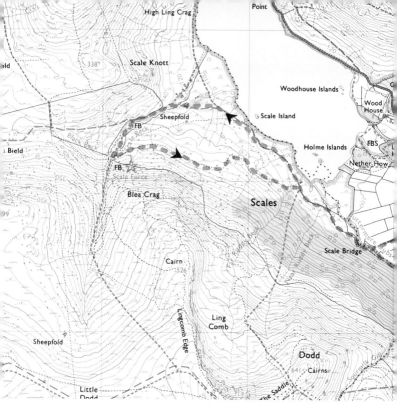

underneath in low water) then turn right towards Crummock Water. This path is followed for 1.5km around the lake, past three small islands and over several wooden footbridges. Look out for the larger footbridge over a stream appearing from a significant cleft between the flanks of Mellbreak and **Blea Crag** – it is in the depths of this cleft that Scale Force is located. Follow the stream up leftwards on either bank to another footbridge after 300m. Take a path on the stream's right, through a gate and cross left on a footbridge over another branch of the stream. Now the path heads steadily upstream to the **waterfall**. Return by the path through the wall on the opposite side of the stream, traversing the hillside above Crummock Water with great views of the Buttermere fells. The path joins the outbound route at the first footbridge at the head of the lake. Retrace your steps to Scale Bridge. Instead of crossing, continue along the path to the bridge at **Sourmilk Gill** on the Buttermere circuit. Turn left, but take the path that follows Buttermere's shore, where there are a series

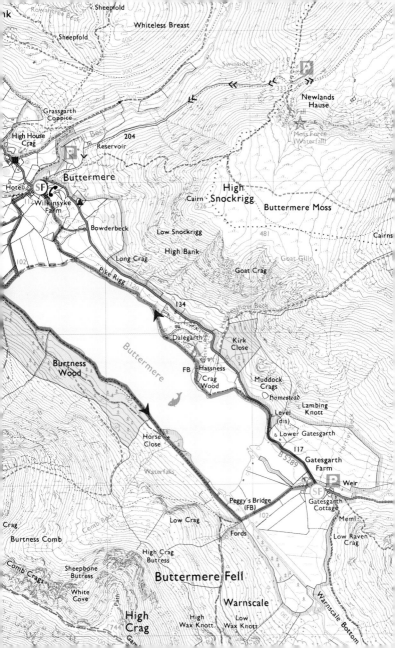

Sheepfold
Whiteless Breast
Sheepfold
Rowan Beck

Grassgarth
Coppice
High House
Crag
204
Reservoir
Buttermere
Hotel
SF
Wilkinsyke
Farm
Bowderbeck
Long Crag
Pike Rigg
Low Snockrigg
High Bank
Goat Crag

Newlands
Hause
Moss Force
(Waterfall)

High
Snockrigg
Cairn
526
Buttermere Moss
481
Cairns
Goat Gills

134
Dalegarth
Kirk
Close
Snow Beck

Burtness
Wood
Buttermere
FB
Hassness
Crag
Wood
Muddock
Crags
Homestead
Lambing
Knott
Level
(dis)
Lower Gatesgarth
Horse
Close
Waterfalls
117
B 5289
Gatesgarth
Farm
P
SF
Weir
Peggy's Bridge
(FB)
Crag
Low Crag
Fords
Gatesgarth
Cottage
Meml

Burtness Comb
Comb Crags
High Crag
Buttress
Sheepbone
Buttress
White Cove
High
Crag
744
Comb Beck
Buttermere Fell
Warnscale
High
Wax Knott
Low
Wax Knott
Low Raven
Crag
Warnscale Bottom

An autumnal evening at Buttermere

of paddling spots on pebble beaches. Continue on the permissive path through the gate along the lakeshore for 500m. At the next gate, turn left on a bridleway that leads around a rocky knoll into **Buttermere village**.

Did you know?

- There are at least five geocaches hidden on the route of the usual Buttermere walk. Lack of mobile phone signal on some networks may cause problems for some geocachers. See Adventure 3 for further information about geocaching.

- There are two rival theories of where the name Buttermere comes from – the first meaning 'lake by the dairy pastures' from the old English and the second after Buthar, an 11th century Viking chieftain.

Adventure 34
Crummock Water – 'Goose Poo' Island and Rannerdale Knotts

Two adventures in one. Water-based fun exploring a small island and ridge top scrambling.

Start/finish	Buttermere area. The beaches and island can be found at NY 166 176 on the B5289. Park considerately here or at the Rannerdale parking area at NY 163 183.
Distance	Woodhouse aka 'Goose Poo' Island lies less than 100m offshore. The Rannerdale route is 6km (3.7 miles) from the island roadside parking or 5km (3.1 miles) from Rannerdale parking with 260m height gain.
Suitable for	● Blue to get onto island, blue for the hike.
Amenities	Cafés and toilets in Buttermere.
Public transport	Bus 77 from Keswick.
Considerations	Rowing boat hire and canoe activities available from Wood House (tel 01768 770 208). Do not get out of your boat at the island if you can see nesting birds. The minimal parking areas and pristine surroundings have sometimes been abused by a growing number of visitors in recent years. Please be considerate and do not add to the problems. Do not light fires or disposable barbecues. If you are lucky enough to own a kayak, please note that officially you need a permit for journeys across the lake. This is available from the machine in Buttermere National Trust car park.

Crummock Water justifiably lays claim to being one of the prettiest spots in the Lake District. Its tempting waters, grass promontories, beaches and spectacular views make it an idyllic swimming and paddling spot. There has traditionally been a tolerant view of families pottering about in inflatable dinghies and kayaks and the shores near the small roadside parking area at the edge of Great Wood are ideal for kids to test their oar skills in shallow water and pay a visit to a tiny island close to shore. Rannerdale Knotts affords tremendous views, has a lovely scrambly ridge crest and a wonderful secluded valley famous for its bluebells. Combining both time on the sparkly water and rocky ridge is the perfect adventurous day.

Setting sail for Goose Poo Island (seen here from the shore of Crummock Water)

Goose Poo Island is the largest of three islands marked as Woodhouse Islands on OS maps. Goose Poo Island, as it is affectionately called by our children, is a more accurate name. Expect to be amazed or appalled at the vast quantities of green goose droppings adorning the vegetated isle and wash your hands after visiting!

Goose Poo Island is clearly seen and easy to row to. A small path by the side of a wall leads from the roadside to the lake and small beaches. There is a long shallow stretch and then deeper water, followed by rocky sections around the island itself. It is surprisingly hard to land on the island, the best places being on its northern tip. Tiny tots will struggle to get out of the boat onto the slippery rocks. If boaters are alighting on the island, make sure that your craft is not going to float off and leave you stranded or with a cold swim back. It is possible to row right around the island but watch out for a shallow rocky channel where the two islets are. At this point, it is often possible for adults and taller children to wade to and from the island without swimming. If doing so, follow the line of the three islands to the shore. An adult should check this route out first and only very strong swimmers should attempt it.

Rannerdale Knotts

If you are starting from the **Rannerdale** parking, follow the path south uphill to gain the steep ridge to the summit. If starting from the roadside parking for the **island**, find a grassy path trending up the hillside parallel to the road. At the ridgeline, take a path steeply uphill to reach the summit at 355m. Go along the obvious ridge south

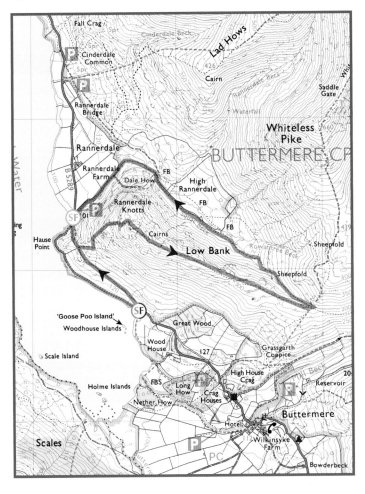

Easter snow – looking north from the Rannerdale ridge

east where there is some superb easy scrambling on the crest. After 1km the ridge descends to a col. Here, turn sharply left to double back down the beautiful mini valley of Rannerdale alongside **Squat Beck**. The path swings left after 1.4km to reach Rannerdale parking. Here, find a path trending uphill to join the outbound route from the roadside island parking.

Bad weather alternative
Paddling can be fun in the rain, but don't take boats out in windy weather.

Adventure 35
The C to C (Children-to-Coast) Challenge

Traffic-free cycling on the famous long-distance
route, paddling on the beach at the end

Start/finish	Ennerdale Bridge area. Rowrah. Layby on A5086 at NY 055 185 at a bend with signs welcoming drivers to Arlecdon. There is a railway bridge and blue cycling sign here.
Distance	26km (16.2 miles) from Rowrah to Whitehaven and back or 13km (8.1 miles) to the sea at Whitehaven only.
Suitable for	● Red. Children capable of cycling 26km on flat good surfaces.
Amenities	Whitehaven. Toilets at James Street.
Public transport	Trains and bike hire in Whitehaven would mean riding the route from the sea
Considerations	Haven Cycles (passed on route) in Whitehaven is open Monday to Saturday and offers cycle hire. The route begins at an elevation of 170m – this is imperceptibly lost on the way to the sea and regained on the return leg – so, dependent on prevailing winds, the return leg will be slightly harder than the outbound one. In Whitehaven, there are short sections on quiet residential roads and a final section on a busier road into town. Younger cyclists could wheel their bikes on the pavement. There are no logical intermediary destinations, but those looking for a shorter totally traffic-free outing will find the cycling most straightforward heading west from Rowrah.

The Children-to-Coast Challenge gives families the chance to sample a fantastic almost wholly traffic-free stretch of Britain's most popular long-distance cycle route – the C2C (Coast to Coast). This route heads west along the C2C from the edges of the Lake District to reach the Irish Sea at the historic fishing town of Whitehaven with its picturesque marina. The North Pier Lighthouse and the nearby Whitehaven Beach make superb destinations for the outbound leg of what is a tremendously satisfying excursion.

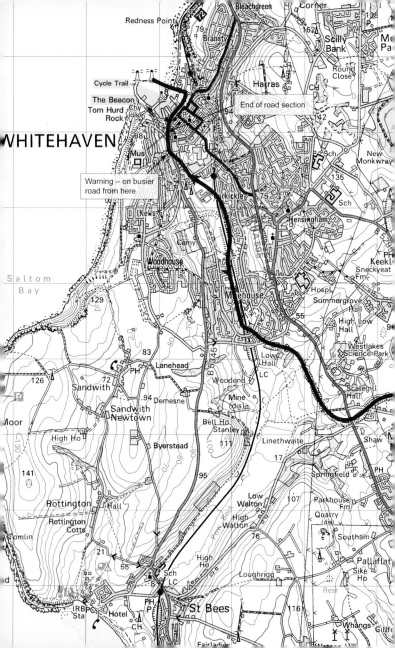

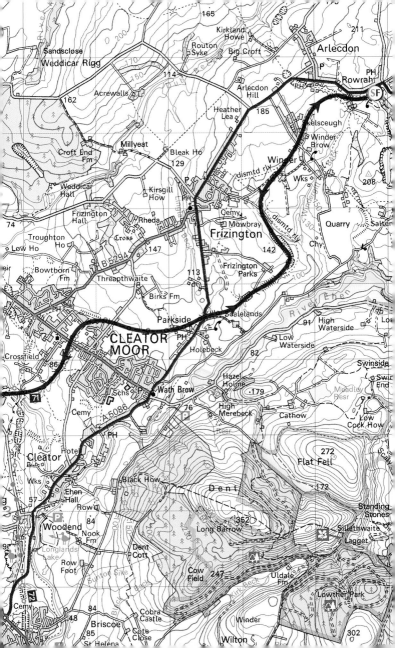

The C2C starts in either Whitehaven or Workington and ends at Tynemouth or Sunderland and was the flagship project of the National Cycle Network devised in 1994. Whitehaven was originally viewed as the alternative start, but proved more popular than Workington.

From the Rowrah layby parking, cross the bridge and turn right down the track to get onto the C2C route. From here the C2C to Whitehaven is easy to follow. Blue metal posts with decorative railway mining trucks that commemorate the area's industrial heritage complement more orthodox signage that will resolve any questions when other cycle paths branch off – simply follow the signs towards Whitehaven. After 1km, good views of Ennerdale appear to your left.

There are various interesting benches along the way, one of which has a poem about the region's mining of coal and iron carved into some red sandstone that is common to the area. Other benches are made from railway sleepers and tracks.

The cycle path along the old railway line eventually leads to a housing estate at **Mirehouse** on the outskirts of Whitehaven proper. There are short passages here on minor residential roads that connect longer sections of traffic-free cycle way (no one will mind if you prefer youngsters to use the pavement). The C2C is well-signed

Leaving the western Lakeland fells behind on the C to C ride

Signs on the old railway route of the C to C ride

and a description of all the turns unnecessary. After passing a rugby pitch to the left of the cycle path you join a quiet road for 100m or so until exiting via a left turn down a cycle path with brilliant S bends – this is the most technical bit of the route. The tunnel into which it leads gives more clearance than it appears, but giants might be wise to duck! After passing the football ground, the cycle paths end near a retail park at a relatively busy town road that amazingly the local authorities have not seen fit to put a cycle lane on. However, you are only 400m from the sea and the pavement can be used without difficulty. At the **Whitehaven Marina** turn right on a wide traffic-free area where there is often an ice cream van – the metal sculpture that marks the beginning of the C2C will be spotted down a ramp. To reach the **North Pier Lighthouse**, continue to the north side of the marina and turn left. There are no fences on the pier, but it is very wide. Continue over weathered sandstone paving to the lighthouse (unless it is temporarily closed for fish being unloaded), noting the path that leads down to **Whitehaven Beach** on the right just after the fishing depot.

To return, reverse the outbound route. Follow signs to **Cleator Moor**, then **Frizington** and continue until **Rowrah** is reached.

Did you know?

- The distinctive candlestick chimney to the south of Whitehaven harbour is a mine shaft chimney built in 1850.

- In May 1910, the Wellington Pit was the scene of Cumbria's worst mining disaster after an explosion and fire led to 132 miners losing their lives.

- Whitehaven beach and nearby cliffs are one of very few locations in the UK where fossils from the Carboniferous era can be found. As long as the tide is out, the beach is a pleasant spot to do some fossil hunting – look for these on the huge rocks that make up the sea wall – and a good location for split parties to meet up.

Adventure 36
Getting to know Loweswater

Walking, paddling, tree climbing and swinging with optional rowing

Start/finish	Loweswater – Maggie's Bridge car park (NY 135 210).
Distance	3km (1.9 miles) or 6km (3.7 miles).
Suitable for	● ● Green. All ages. The short option is easy and flat and very young children will manage it. The longer blue alternative is steeper.
Amenities	The Kirkstile Inn in Loweswater has a beer garden and serves hot chocolate, and there is a tea room on the road to Lorton and in Lorton village shop.
Considerations	Loweswater occasionally has blue-green algae in its water. Take notice of any warning signs that have been posted. Although using your own boats is prohibited on Loweswater, the National Trust-owned rowing boats at Watergate Farm are available for hire (tel 01946 861465).

Loweswater is one of the Lake District's hidden gems being the northernmost link in the lovely chain that includes Buttermere (which it was once joined to) and Crummock Water. It is a great option for a shorter or rainy day activity with the children. There is an easy path and plenty to entertain young adventurers on route. The three wooden rope swings which arc out almost over the water towards the dramatic fells are usually crowd-pleasers. Some excellent trees to climb and pebbly beaches for paddling and skimming add to the attractions, and for older or more energetic children, there's the chance to climb up to a hidden wooded waterfall and traverse a secluded valley across the slopes of Burnbank Fell high above the lake. Loweswater is a great place to spot red squirrels, cormorants and grebes.

Take the track out of the car park over a cattle grid and cross a small bridge at **Dub Beck** – a good pooh sticks spot. After 200m there are some great twisted trees for climbing on the right. Continue for 700m to meet the lakeshore near **Watergate Farm**. There are some nice beaches here for paddling. Go through a gate into **Holme Wood** and follow the well-made path through the shoreline woods to reach the stone cottage of Holme Wood Bothy after 600m. Here, there are pebble beaches with great rope tree swings which catapult children right out over the lake. There are good climbing trees in the area.

A little further along the lakeshore path from the bothy, you might spot a rectangular platform near the shore. This was used in World War 2 when cables where stretched across the lake to prevent landings by incoming German sea planes.

For the shorter route, retrace your steps back to the car park.

Blue option

This longer and higher route works best using the lakeshore option to return. Go through the gate opposite the car park on a track to **High Nook Farm**. Go through the farmyard and bear slightly left on a track gaining height in a hidden cirque

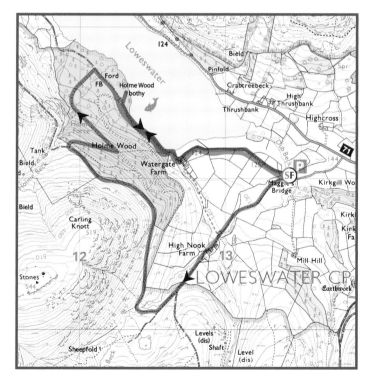

Swinging in the rain at Loweswater

The large twisted climbing tree near Maggie's Bridge

containing the tiny High Nook Tarn. Swing right before the tarn on a good path which formed part of the Corpse Road from Buttermere to Lamplugh church and on to the coast. This follows a wall and allows views over the lake at gaps in the woodland. Before meeting the watercourse of **Holme Beck**, look out for a small gate in the wall. Go right steeply downhill through this then turn sharply left after 300m on a forest track, which leads to the secret waterfall of **Holme Force** at a bridge. Continue down the track for 400m to turn right on the lakeshore path to return to **Maggie's Bridge**.

Bad weather alternative
Don the waterproofs and wellies – this route is fine in the rain.

Did you know?

- Holme Wood bothy is not a bothy as the word is used in this book. It is a basic cottage owned by the National Trust available for hire for up to six people.
- Some of the buoys floating in the lake emit ultrasound waves as part of an ongoing project to curb the periodic blooms of algae at Loweswater.

Adventure 37
Sale Fell and its bouldering wall

A grassy fell climb with a natural climbing wall at the top

Start/finish	Embleton area– the small parking area at St Margaret's Church in Wythop Mill (NY 190 301).
Distance	3.2km (2 miles) with 240m ascent.
Suitable for	● Blue – one of the easier blue fell routes. Most four-year-olds will manage the walking and climbing and it will be a doddle for older children.
Amenities	Bassenthwaite or Cockermouth.
Public transport	Bus X4 and X5 from Keswick to within 2km of start.
Considerations	Sale Fell can be windy. The fell-top crag is great for bouldering but younger climbers will need watching at the crag's edge and spotting by an adult ready to prevent a tumble. The grassy paths can be slippery in the rain.

Peak-bagging and practising climbing moves can be combined on a visit to the graceful grassy summit slopes of Sale Fell. At 359m, this modest outlying hill is the north-westernmost outpost of the National Park and one of the 214 sought-after Wainwright summits. It has wonderful sea and mountain views and makes a perfect first proper Lakeland fell to climb with the kids. It was one of our then three-year-old daughter's first Wainwrights. The exciting objective of a natural children's climbing wall at the top has made it somewhere she wants to keep coming back to. This circular walk to Sale Fell is all on broad grassy paths of a relatively friendly gradient. In late summer, families can forage for bilberries and compete for who can get the bluest tongues. Sale Fell is far enough off the beaten track to attract relatively few ramblers, even in sunny school holidays.

Go through the gate into the **church graveyard** (the church is open and worth a look inside) and back out at the top left-hand corner. From the convenient bench here, go leftwards then after 100m, turn sharply right to join the main large grassy track up the fell. Head up rightwards more gradually now between forests of ferns, winding around the fell-side with views to Bassenthwaite behind you. After 600m at a junction of paths by a wall, take the left-hand option striking up the broad ridge towards the summit. The undulating path leading to the unmarked fell top gives unparalleled sea views. Take note of the small **crag** just before the summit. This is best accessed by

'I'll race you to the top' – on the grassy flanks of Sale Fell

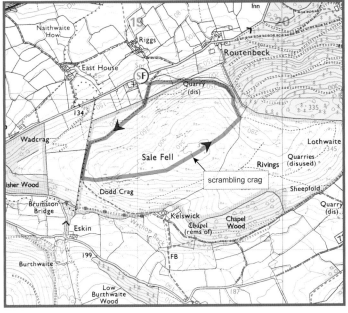

Ready to stop a slip at the top of Sale Fell

walking round from the top. Aspiring alpinists can hone their skills here. The easier lines are to the middle and right of the mini-face. Older kids can have a go at the steeper rock on the left. Some prudent spotting from the adults is necessary.

From the top, continue north-east along the path and descend easily to a wall bounding the large **Wythop Woods**. Turn left and follow the wall more steeply down to where a path traverses back left again to skirt around the bilberry covered flanks of the fell and eventually rejoin the main path above the church. Either return through the graveyard or follow the path swinging rightwards to reach the road by way of an alternative track.

Bad weather alternative
Do it anyway and then go to dry off in a café in Cockermouth. In really poor visibility, retrace your steps from the summit.

Did you know?

- The summit climbing wall is made from unusually beautiful pink-tinged Ordovician rock.

- Scotland, the Isle of Man, Skiddaw and Helvellyn can all be spotted from Sale Fell's summit ridge.

Adventure 38
Maryport coastal journey

Riding to Allonby beach on the coastal path, exploring rock pools and crabbing from the quay

Start/finish	Maryport. The free promenade parking at the end of Strand Road (NY 037 374) just out of town is the best place to start cycling. There is also paid parking at the harbour (NY 032 366).
Distance	14km (8.7 miles) for the full ride. There are many shorter options.
Suitable for	⚫ ⚫ All families – as much or as little of the ride can be done as you like (green). The full ride is blue. Scooters, pushchairs and pedestrians can all enjoy the promenade.
Amenities	Maryport has cafés and an excellent maritime-themed public playground behind the aquarium. There are toilets at the aquarium and Wave Centre. Allonby has a tea room open Wednesday–Sunday, the 'Codfather' fish-and-chip shop, pubs, and an ice cream shop. There are public toilets at the seafront playground.
Public transport	Maryport is on the Cumbrian Coast rail line. It is also served by bus from Whitehaven and Cockermouth
Considerations	Extra close supervision should be given to children near drops from the harbour walls and quays. Seaweed-draped rocks on the seashore can be slippery. Check tide times as there is not much sand at high tide. Wash hands after going on the beach or crabbing. On the cycle ride, take care at the two crossings of the fast B5300. Bike hire is available if you start at Allonby (tel 07551 750373).

Maryport and Allonby's excellent extensive seaside cycling combined with miles of mixed sand, shingle and rock-pooled beaches have made this adventure a hit with our children. The working fishing town of Maryport is unpretentious, uncrowded and surprisingly accessible from northern Lakeland. Quayside crab-catching at the harbour or lighthouse will be a hit with some children, whereas others may prefer searching the red sandstone pools on the beach for crabs, small crayfish or anemones. The cycle ride takes the National Cycle

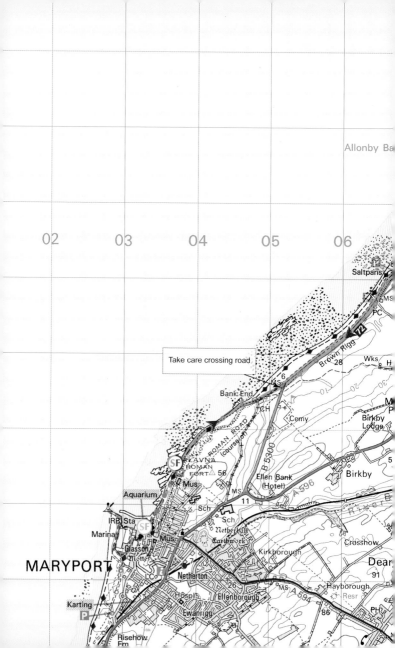

Take care crossing road

Network's Route 72, Hadrian's Cycleway, up the historic and unpopulated Solway Coast to the beachfront village of Allonby. The ride is flat and is a good choice for building children's cycling stamina without off-putting inclines. As a bonus, the sea is never out of view – pack beach gear and stop off wherever takes your fancy. You are guaranteed to find your own deserted expanse at low tide. This stretch of the Cumbrian coast is not actually part of the Lake District National Park but has been designated as an area of outstanding natural beauty. It can also be a breath of fresh air; there is always a bracing breeze and it often stays dry here when it is raining further inland.

Begin at the **seafront parking areas** at the end of Strand Road. From here, simply get on the wide promenade and cycle away from town up the coast, with lovely flower-strewn bluffs to the right and views across the Solway Firth to Scotland on the left. After 2km, at **Maryport Golf Club**, very young cyclists may wish to turn back. A long-term diversion (follow

> The shores by the start of the route are the best for rock pooling. Closer to Allonby, there is a greater proportion of sand.

blue 72 signs with Roman centurion heads) along the club access road for 100m means that an occasional golfer's car may be on route.

Dismount to cross the **B5300** with care and continue on the traffic-free tarmac path right of the road and separated from it by flora, which fortuitously blocks the road from view but still lets cyclists see the sea. After 1.5km, take care where the path crosses a tiny road to **Crosscanonby**. There is parking for visitors to the **Roman Mile Fortlet 21** here. Should you wish to visit this, follow the footpath gently uphill for 10 minutes to reach a vantage point for the UK's first fully excavated mile fortlet. The footprint of the structure is easily discernible. If that diversion doesn't seem enticing, look out 200m or so further along the cycle path opposite the apex of the Fortlet Hill, where a grassy access path back across the B5300 leads immediately to the 10m wide circular walled depression of an Elizabethan **salt pan**. Sea salt for preserving food was collected in this area for 700 years.

In less than 1km, the cycle path crosses back over the B road and continues on a gravelly path through the dunes with increasingly sandy beaches on the left, arriving at **Allonby** in another 2.5km. Allonby's public toilets and children's playground are 200m further up the coast. Return by the outbound route.

It is possible to continue the ride into Maryport past the aquarium and right around the harbour and marina to Maryport lighthouse. There might be an occasional vehicle on this extended part of the route. The octagonal lighthouse is one of the oldest cast iron lighthouses in the world and features in several paintings by 'matchstick man' LS Lowry.

Coastal cycling past the red sandstone on the beach at Maryport

Maryport

The Roman name for Maryport was Alauna. As the site of an important fort built at the same time as Hadrian's Wall, there is plenty to interest young historians here.

The remains of a Roman fort on the Cumbrian coastal frontier can be seen on the hilltop by the start of the route beside the Senhouse Roman Museum (it is well marked with brown signs from the town centre). Roman Mile Fortlet 21 can also be visited on the ride to Allonby.

Bad weather alternative

The Lake District Coast Aquarium in town is a sure-fire winner. The Maritime museum showcases the town's links to famous ships such as the *Titanic* and the *Bounty* and the Senhouse museum explains the town's Roman heritage. The Wave Centre on the harbour has climbing walls and indoor caving.

Crabbing

Crabbing nets, lines and bait can be purchased from the shop inside the Lake District Coast Aquarium in the harbour.

Even at low tide, it is usually possible to find somewhere to dangle a line. The harbour wall directly in front of the aquarium has a reassuring railing or the pier just by the lighthouse is a good spot for crabbing. Take extra care as there are long drops down to the water.

Crabbing, like most fishing, benefits from a patient approach. Crabs can be carefully picked up and inspected using a finger and thumb from behind on their underside and back – well out of reach of their pincers – before being returned to the sea.

Young crabber and his catch at Maryport harbour

Adventure 39
Bassenthwaite Lake: ospreys, Dodd Wood and Mirehouse

Birdwatching, hiking, climbing a fell, adventure trails and building dens

Start/finish	Bassenthwaite – Dodd Wood car park or laybys nearby off the A591 (NY 236 282).
Distance	Main blue route 3.5km (2.2 miles); extended blue route 6km (3.7 miles).
Suitable for	● ● Blue, but there are options for all ages, including a green option of just 1km to the osprey-viewing area and around Mirehouse Gardens.
Amenities	The Old Sawmill tearoom by the car park.
Public transport	Bus 73 from Keswick.
Considerations	This route straddles the A591. Take care crossing from the car park. A part of the extended walk through Mirehouse Gardens and their charming wooded playgrounds has a charge (£4 per adult and £2 per child) but a free alternative route is also described. Osprey sightings are not guaranteed. Check www.ospreywatch.co.uk for up-to-date information. Using a telescope (even with lots of help) is a skill and under 4s will struggle to focus on what's in sight. There is a video feed of the nest at the platform that should help avoid frustration. The trails in Dodd Wood are relatively short but quite steep at the start.

Birdwatching may not sound like every parent's idea of a family adventure but you might be surprised to find that you have a budding twitcher in your midst. In fact, the majestic sight of one of the extremely rare and massive white-chested ospreys, which have nested near Bassenthwaite Lake since 2001, will capture the imagination of adults and children alike. With the help of ornithologist volunteers at the free viewing platform, train your telescopes onto the nesting birds of prey – they are easily seen feeding and fishing in the lake for trout, roach and perch most days from April to August. Combine the birding with a mushroom-spotting competition among the towering pines of the peaceful Dodd Wood. Scull about the pebbly banks of Skill Beck and explore the adventure trails near the lakeshore in the grounds of Mirehouse. Energetic families can challenge themselves with an extended route climbing right to the top of Dodd Fell – a Wainwright peak much maligned by the man himself who was famously not fond of manmade forests.

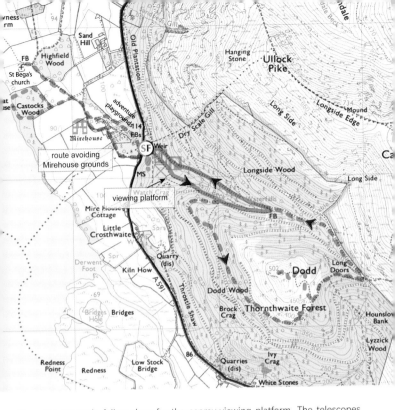

From the car park, follow signs for the osprey-viewing platform. The telescopes are manned by volunteers daily from April to September. They will help children to train their sights on the birds nesting down below on the shores of Bassenthwaite and have lots of information about the impressive birds. There are often red squirrels scurrying to and from their nests in this area too. Just before the viewing platform at a bend with a picnic table, there is a great spot for building woodland dens from cut branches. Children can construct a tepee structure around the base of a pine tree.

From the viewing platform, double back 100m and turn right up the **Skill Beck** trail. The trail takes walkers steeply up one side of the beck through the mixed woodland and back down the other using shady paths strewn with pine needles and wider forest tracks. The trail is well signed with red arrows. There are a few pleasant paddling spots on the initial section.

The trail crosses the **beck** on a wooden footbridge and is signed down the other side of the ravine in the hillside and back to the car park and the Old Sawmill café.

Dodd Wood

Building a den in Dodd Wood

Dodd Wood's damp and dappled floor seems to be prime fungus territory. Poisonous-looking mushrooms abound. Do not touch these, but children can have fun spotting and photographing different kinds and trying to work out who has found the most toxic one by using the internet later on.

Pine cones are plentiful here. It should be possible to find at least three distinct types as larch, Scots pine, Douglas fir and Norway and Sitka spruce all grow in the woods. Dodd Wood is owned by the Forestry Commission and some of its towering pines were originally planted in the 1920s.

Extended route

For a modest amount of extra effort, it is possible to climb out of the forest to the open summit of Dodd Fell. At the top of the steep part of the hill, the Dodd Fell trail splits off right from the **Skill Beck** one. It is well signed and gives great views of Bassenthwaite and the Skiddaw group fells as it turns left up a wide ridge to the heathery summit area. The last 350m to the summit should be retraced, then a well signed circular descent route is followed, joining the Skill Beck trail again before the wooden bridge.

To avoid Mirehouse Gardens, cross the road from the car park and head down the path to the left of the Mirehouse entrance to visit the beautifully situated **St Bega's church**, where there is unofficial access to the lakeshore.

Mirehouse

Tickets for the Mirehouse Gardens must be purchased at the café. If you plan to go in, cross the road carefully from the parking area and enter the **Mirehouse** grounds, continuing on a short circular walk through the lovely wooded rhododendron gardens, which are interspersed with lots of hidden adventurous play areas to find with challenges for children of all ages and a great aerial glide. The whole thing is a remarkably subtle take on woodland adventure playgrounds and is always quiet.

It is possible to do a lakeside walk on land owned by Mirehouse. This adds another 1.5km to the route and, despite its name, the walk is rarely on the lake's side, though it is possible to get onto pebbly beaches at a few points.

St Bega's is a restored Norman church only accessible on foot. Its unique setting near the lakeshore and framed by the flanks of Skiddaw provided literary inspiration for both Wordsworth and Tennyson.

Bad weather alternative

Rain won't stop the ospreys and it shouldn't stop you. Take shelter in the tearoom or pay a little extra to visit the interior of Mirehouse – the historic home of the Spedding family.

St Bega's Church on the shores of Bassenthwaite

The splendid approach via Dash Falls

Adventure 40
Overnight at the loneliest house – Skiddaw

Backpacking to stay at a remote youth hostel, visiting Whitewater Dash fall, options to climb Skiddaw or Blencathra

Start/finish	Bassenthwaite area – the parking area opposite Peter House Farm (NY 249 323), which is 2km (1.2 miles) off the A591.
Distance	5.6km (3.5 miles) to hostel with 250m ascent. Same distance for return. Skiddaw summit is 3.6km (2.2 miles) with 480m ascent from the hostel and Blencathra is 5.2km (3.2 miles) with 450m ascent. Double the distances for the return trips.
Suitable for	● Red. The backpacking adventure can be manageable for most families with thorough planning. It is on a good track. Parents have reportedly even got an all-terrain pushchair to Skiddaw House by this route. The ascent of Skiddaw from the hostel is much harder going and that of Blencathra harder still. Families with older children who are very strong cyclists could consider biking to the hostel (black).
Amenities	The hostel has a 'shop' where DIY breakfasts, packed lunches and dinners can be bought. Parents may also be interested in the small but well-stocked bar.
Public transport	Keswick. It is possible to hike 8km along the Cumbrian Way from Keswick to reach Skiddaw House (red).
Considerations	Skiddaw House is off-grid. It has solar-powered lighting, log fires and gas-fired showers and cookers. There are no sockets, no phone signal and no Wi-Fi. This is only recommended for families as a summer outing. It is also possible to camp at Skiddaw House.

If you truly want to give your children an experience of staying overnight in a slightly spooky and remote mountain setting, you couldn't ask for a better excursion than this. Skiddaw House stands in proud isolation high on the eastern slopes of the mountain which is its namesake. It is a 22-bed youth hostel, which is 5.6km from the nearest proper road. The beauty of this adventure is that it is a challenging but achievable objective for most families in summer and a fantastic introduction to backpacking. The track to the hostel from Peterhouse Farm is easy underfoot and simple to navigate in iffy weather (it is a much more serious prospect in winter). Families need only take the bare essentials as the hostel sells food and provides bedding. This means that the trip can be a viable option for parents of younger children who may need carrying part of the way. Should none of this persuade you, there is plenty more to recommend the outing: at 470m, Skiddaw House makes an excellent higher altitude base for children to make a bid for the summits of both Skiddaw (931m) and Blencathra (868m). Families with older children looking for a serious challenge can camp in the hostel grounds or even try mountain-biking up the track to get there. The hike up to Skiddaw House is exceptional in itself, passing the impressive drops of the falls of Whitewater Dash en route.

Follow the signed bridleway gradually uphill on tarmac initially. After a mile, the track splits, with our route signed rightwards. Continue rising gradually, arcing around the hillside under **Dead Crags**, with the innocuous-looking **Dash Beck** in the valley bottom. The **waterfalls** at the head of the valley soon become visible and the track leads up to them, with a steep section curving up the side of the falls (take care if you venture off the wide track towards the precipitous edge of the falls). Above the falls, the track crosses the beck and contours the lower slopes of **Great Calva**. When it comes into view **Skiddaw House** is bleakly obvious – the only dwelling for miles around. The building itself is rather grey and unlovely, but it draws the eye, partly due to being

The destination in sight – the lonely youth hostel beneath the steep slopes of Lonscale Fell

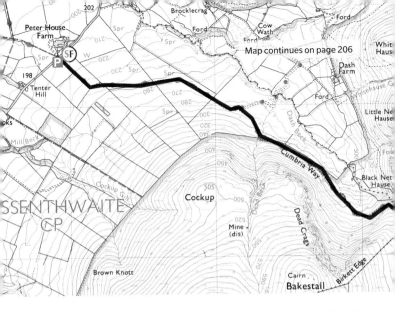

Map continues on page 206

set in an incongruous copse of wind-battered spindly trees; it is a rather eerie sight. Follow the track, slightly dropping and rising again to the building, whose warm and welcoming interior might be a comforting thought if the weather has been as wild as it can be on the Back o' Skiddaw.

Option B: Ascent of Skiddaw – red

There are pros and cons to taking children up this route from the hostel. The pros are it is not terribly steep and it is soft going underfoot. The downside is that it can often be boggy, but the pay-off is reaching the top of one of England's highest mountains from an unusually high starting point.

At the hostel gate, turn immediately left hiking gradually uphill on a grassy and often boggy path to eventually reach **Sale How** with its satanic 666m spot height and views of Skiddaw if the weather allows. Descend slightly from the unmarked top and then continue on the same path climbing still gradually for another mile to reach a fence boundary and meet a major path up Skiddaw from **Little Man**. Turn right on this, crossing a stile and climbing more steeply on a better rockier path over a few false tops to **Skiddaw summit** (trig point) in 900m.

Option C: Ascent of Blencathra – red

This is a far more adventurous and harder choice of summit. The pay-off again is reaching one of the highest and most famous summits in England. There is no path

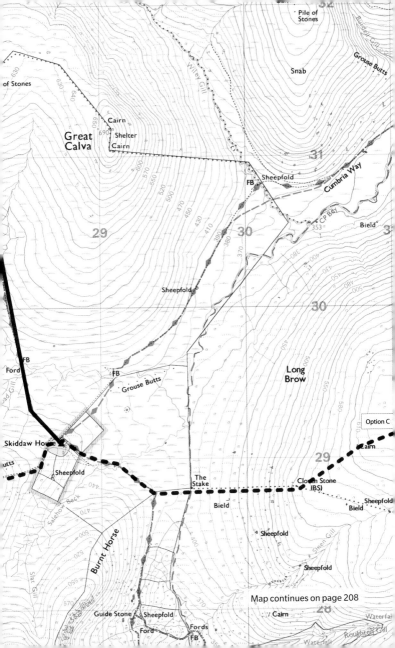

Pile of Stones

Snab

Grouse Butts

of Stones

Cairn

Great
Calva

Shelter
Cairn

31

Witey Gill

Cumbria Way

FB   Sheepfold

29

CP Bdy   353

Bield

30

Sheepfold

30

Long
Brow

FB
Ford

FB

Grouse Butts

Option C

Cairn

Skiddaw House

29

utts

Sheepfold

The
Stake

Clough Stone
(BS)

Sheepfold

Bield

Bield

Burnt Horse

Salehow Beck

Sheepfold

Sheen Gill

Sheepfold

Map continues on page 208

Guide Stone   Sheepfold

Ford

Fords
FB

Cairn

Waterfall

Roughten Gill

Waterfall

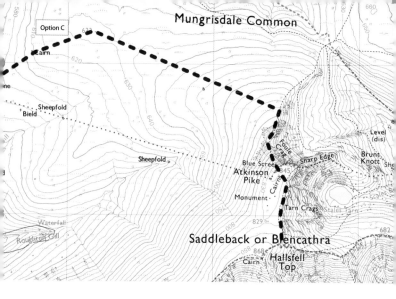

on the map but it does exist (albeit faint and squelchy) on the ground, largely thanks to fell runners. Navigation is harder on this route and it is not recommended in poor visibility. The route is slightly more interesting than the one to Skiddaw, with a spot of bouldering on the Cloven Stone and views of the dramatic cliffs of Foule Crag and Sharp Edge adding excitement.

Turn right on the bridleway below the hostel and descend to cross a stream after 300m. Continue for a further 200m through a gate in a fence. Here, turn left beside the fence and continue on a faint path in this direction over a short boggy section then climbing more steeply to reach the **Cloven Stone** (a 2m high boulder shaped like a cloven hoof) after 900m. The path continues upwards in an east-north-easterly direction to reach a tall **cairn** after 500m. Continue in the same direction to reach another cairn in 300m. This marks the top of the otherwise unremarkable **Mungrisdale Common** at 633m (a Wainwright summit believe it or not!). From here, follow the largest path east-south-east towards Blencathra's summit ridge, where the steep slope of **Atkinson Pike** guards the way. After a flattish mile, the gradient steepens dramatically to gain the summit ridge at the cairn of Atkinson Pike above the termination of Sharp Edge. A choice of paths leads south in 400m to **Blencathra's summit**.

Bad weather alternative

Rooms at Skiddaw House must be booked in advance so the weather will be a gamble. Take waterproofs and relish the challenge of getting there in driving rain – it will make the hot chocolate and log fire all the more well deserved when you arrive.

Otherworldy evening light at the loneliest house

Skiddaw House was built in 1829. It was formerly used as a shooting lodge and a shepherd's bothy before falling into disuse and being reopened as the highest YHA bunkhouse in Britain. The hostel aims to have a low impact on its mountain environment. It has fleece insulated walls and uses solar panels to generate electricity. Wood stoves are fuelled from the coppice and there is spring-fed water. Somewhat surprisingly, Skiddaw House seems to be a ghost-free zone. It was, however, the scene of a fictional foul murder committed by the evil Uhland in a 1920s Hugh Walpole novel.

Did you know?

- Blencathra is the legendary resting place of King Arthur and his knights. They are said to be lying dormant inside the mountain but will rise again if the mountain should ever come under attack in the future.

Appendix A
Routes by activity

Adventures		Grade	Page
CYCLING 🚲			
Adventure 2	Great Langdale Bike Trail, Elterwater and Skelwith Force	⬤⬤	44
Adventure 8	Castle to castle at Windermere	⬤⬤	71
Adventure 10	Grizedale Forest – Mushrooms and Wild Art	⬤⬤	78
Adventure 12	Hodbarrow Lagoon and Haverigg lighthouses	⬤	84
Adventure 15	Ride the Esk Trail to the sea	⬤	95
Adventure 19	A wild Ennerdale journey to Black Sail	⬤⬤	113
Adventure 23	Taking on Whinlatter's Quercus Trail	⬤⬤	131
Adventure 25	Riding on Keswick's old railway	⬤	139
Adventure 35	The C-to-C (Children-to-Coast) Challenge	⬤	181
Adventure 38	Maryport coastal journey	⬤⬤	193
ON THE WATER 🚣 ⛵			
Adventure 1	Swallows and Amazons Island, Coniston	⬤	40
Adventure 9	Gummer's How and Fell Foot Park	⬤	74
Adventure 14	Kail Pot and Hardnott Roman Fort	⬤	91
Adventure 21	Squirrel Nutkin's Island, Derwent Water	⬤	124
Adventure 26	Ullswater's four island challenge	⬤⬤⬤	143
Adventure 28	Galleny Force and Smithymire Island	⬤	151
Adventure 34	Crummock Water: 'Goose Poo' Island and Rannerdale Knotts	⬤	177
MOUNTAIN CLIMB ⛰ ✏			
Adventure 6	The Lion and the Lamb – Helm Crag and Grasmere	⬤	62
Adventure 9	Gummer's How and Fell Foot Park	⬤	74
Adventure 11	Hampsfell and its curious Hospice	⬤	81
Adventure 13	Stickle Pike – a big mountain in miniature	⬤	88
Adventure 17	Meet the Old Man of Coniston	⬤⬤	105

Adventures		Grade	Page
Adventure 18	Pavey Ark and Stickle Ghyll scramble	●	109
Adventure 20	Scafell Pike – An Adventurer's Way	●●●	118
Adventure 22	Catbells and Derwent Water	●	127
Adventure 30	The Bowder Stone and King's How	●●	159
Adventure 31	Jopplety How and Watendlath	●●	163
Adventure 32	Castle Crag and the Cave Hotel	●●	167
Adventure 34	Crummock Water: 'Goose Poo' Island and Rannerdale Knotts	●	177
Adventure 37	Sale Fell and its bouldering wall	●	190
OVERNIGHT STAY 🅐			
Adventure 5	Mosedale Cottage Backpacking	●	58
Adventure 19	A wild Ennerdale journey to Black Sail	●	113
Adventure 29	Buttermere Bothying – Dubs Hut and Warnscale Head	●●	154
Adventure 40	Overnight at the loneliest house – Skiddaw	●	203
HIKING 🚶			
Adventure 3	Tarn Hows geocaching	●●	49
Adventure 4	Cathedral Caves	●	53
Adventure 7	Rydal Caves and Loughrigg	●●●	66
Adventure 14	Kail Pot and Hardnott Roman Fort	●	91
Adventure 16	The Fickle Steps of Dunnerdale	●●	100
Adventure 24	Castlerigg Stone Circular	●	135
Adventure 27	The cascades of Aira Force	●	149
Adventure 28	Galleny Force and Smithymire Island	●	151
Adventure 33	Buttermere and Scale Force	●	172
Adventure 36	Getting to know Loweswater	●●	186
Adventure 39	Bassenthwaite Lake: ospreys, Dodd Wood and Mirehouse	●	198

Appendix B

Where to hire bikes and boats

BIKES

Allonby
Solway Cycle Hire
Sea Banks
CA15 6PT
07551 750373
www.solwaycyclehire.co.uk

Ambleside
Ghyllside Cycles
The Slack
LA22 9DQ
01539 433592
www.ghyllside.co.uk

Coniston
Coniston Boating Centre also hires bikes
(see listing in Appendix C)

Eskdale
West Lakes Adventure
Boot
CA19 1TH
01946 723753
www.westlakesadventure.co.uk

Grasmere
Thorney How
Helm Close
LA22 9AW
01539 435597
www.thorneyhow.co.uk

Grizedale Forest
Grizedale Mountain Bikes
LA22 0QJ
01229 860335
www.grizedalemountainbikes.co.uk

Keswick
Keswick Bike Shop
133 Main St
CA12 5NJ
01768 775202
www.keswickbikes.co.uk

E-Venture Bikes
Elliot Park
CA12 5NZ
07783 822722
www.e-venturebikes.co.uk

Whinlatter Bikes
32 Main Street
CA12 5DX
01768 773940
www.whinlatterbikes.com

Ulverston
Lake District Bikes
Lowick
LA12 8DX
07887 731552
www.lakedistrictbikes.com

Whinlatter Forest
Cyclewise
Whinlatter Pass
CA12 5TW
01768 778711
www.cyclewise.co.uk

Windermere
Country Lanes Cycle Centre
Station Precinct
LA23 1AH
www.countrylaneslakedistrict.co.uk

Lake District Bike Hire
Chestnut Road
LA23 2AL
07932 954530
www.lakedistrictbikehire.co.uk

Windermere Canoe and Kayak also hires
bikes (see listing in Appendix C)

Brockhole Centre
LA23 1LJ
01539 446601
www.brockhole.co.uk

Whitehaven

Haven Cycles
2 Preston St
CA28 9DL
01946 63263
www.havencycles-c2cservices.co.uk

BOATS

Coniston Water

Coniston Boating Centre
Lake Road
Coniston
LA21 8EW
01539 441366
www.conistonboatingcentre.co.uk

Crummock Water

Rowing boats and canoe activities
at Wood House
CA13 9FG
01768 770208
www.woodhousebuttermere.uk

Derwent Water

Nichol End Marine
Portinscale
CA12 5TY
01768 773082
www.nicholend.co.uk

Derwent Water Marina
Portinscale
CA12 5RF
01768 772912
www.getonthelake.co.uk

Ullswater

St Patrick's Boat Landings
Glenridding
CA11 0QQ
01768 482393
www.stpatricksboatlandings.co.uk

Glenridding Sailing Centre
Glenridding
CA11 0PE
01768 482541
www.glenriddingsailingcentre.co.uk

Windermere

Windermere Canoe and Kayak
B5285
Windermere
LA23 3JH
01539 444451
www.windermerecanoekayak.com

Brockhole
(see listing in Appendix B)

Fell Foot Park
(row boats from National Trust café April–
September)
Windermere
Fell Foot Park
seasonal kayaks and stand-up paddle-
boards from Total Adventure
01539 443151
www.total-adventure.co.uk

Loweswater

Rowing boats from Watergate Farm
CA13 0RU
01946 861465

Appendix C
Attractions and playgrounds

INDOOR AND PAID ATTRACTIONS – SOUTHERN LAKES

Ambleside
Wray Castle
www.nationaltrust.org.uk

Bowness
The World of Beatrix Potter
www.hop-skip-jump.com

Coniston
John Ruskin Museum
www.ruskinmuseum.com

Grange-over-Sands
Holker Hall
www.holker.co.uk

Grasmere
Dove Cottage
www.wordsworth.org.uk

Hawkshead
The Beatrix Potter Museum and Hill Top
www.nationaltrust.org.uk

Kendal
Lakeland Maze Farm Park
www.lakelandmaze.co.uk

Sizergh Castle
www.nationaltrust.org.uk

Newby Bridge
Lakeland Motor Museum
www.lakelandmotormuseum.co.uk

Lakeside and Haverthwaite Railway
www.lakesiderailway.co.uk

Ravenglass
Muncaster Castle Hawk and Owl Centre
www.muncaster.co.uk

Ravenglass and Eskdale Railway
www.ravenglass-railway.co.uk

Ulverston
South Lakes Safari Zoo
www.southlakessafarizoo.com

Windermere
The Lakes Aquarium
www.lakesaquarium.co.uk

INDOOR AND PAID ATTRACTIONS – NORTHERN LAKES

Bassenthwaite
Lake District Wildlife Park
www.lakedistrictwildlifepark.co.uk

Mirehouse
www.mirehouse.co.uk

Cockermouth
Wordsworth House and Gardens
www.nationaltrust.org.uk

Cockermouth Leisure Centre
www.better.org.uk

Honister Slate Mine
www.honister.com

Keswick
Keswick Leisure Centre
www.better.org.uk

The Puzzling Place
www.puzzlingplace.co.uk

The Pencil Museum
www.derwentart.com

Keswick Museum and Art Gallery
www.keswickmuseum.org.uk

Keswick Climbing Wall
www.keswickclimbingwall.co.uk

Keswick Kong Adventure climbing wall
www.kongadventure.com

Maryport
Lake District Coast Aquarium
www.coastaquarium.co.uk

Wave Centre climbing wall
www.better.org.uk

West Coast Indoor Karting
www.westcoastkarting.co.uk

Penrith
Rheged Centre
www.rheged.com

Lowther Castle and Lakeland Bird of Prey
Centre
www.lowthercastle.org

Threlkeld
Threlkeld Mining Museum
www.threlkeldquarryandminingmuseum.co.uk

PLAYGROUNDS
These are free to use but there may be
parking charges at some of them.

Cockermouth
Memorial Gardens
CA13 0HR

Harris Park
CA13 0DR

Whinlatter
Forest centre

Keswick
Fitz Park
Station Road
CA12 4NF

Grizedale
Forest centre

Grasmere
Broadgate
LA22 9TA

Ambleside
Rothay Park
LA22 9DH

Windermere
Langrigge Drive
LA23 3AH

Queen's Park
LA23 2AW

Newby Bridge
Fell Foot Park

Brockhole visitor centre
LA23 1LJ

Eskdale
Dalegarth station
CA19 1TG

Ravenglass
near station
CA18 1SW

Maryport
Shiver Me Timbers
South Quay
CA15 8AB

Whitehaven
Castle Park
CA28 7RA

Appendix D
Outdoor activity providers

Although the intention of this guidebook is to allow families to organise their own outdoor adventures, the following companies can be useful for trying new technical pursuits such as rock-climbing and abseiling or harder scrambling. They can also provide watersports instruction including sailing and white water kayaking. None of them have been tested by the authors.

Coniston Boating Centre
Coniston LA21 9EW
www.conistonboatingcentre.co.uk

Derwent Water Marina
Keswick CA12 5RF
www.derwentwatermarina.co.uk

Glaramara Outdoor Adventures
Borrowdale CA12 5XQ
www.glaramara.co.uk

Glenridding Sailing Centre CA11 0PE
www.glenriddingsailingcentre.co.uk

Go Ape has high ropes courses at Whinlatter and Grizedale
www.goape.co.uk

Galloway Wild Foods runs Lakeland mushroom foraging sessions
www.gallowaywildfoods.com

Honister via ferrata CA12 5XN
www.honister.com

Keswick Adventure Centre CA12 4NL
www.keswickadventurecentre.co.uk

Keswick Canoe and Bushcraft CA12 4TT

Keswick Climbing Wall and Outdoor Adventure Centre CA12 4RN
www.keswickclimbingwall.co.uk

Keswick Extreme
Nichol End CA12 5TY
www.keswickextreme.com

Lakeland Ascents operates in Langdale
www.lakelandascents.co.uk

Mobile Adventure
Cockermouth CA13 0QE
www.mobileadventure.co.uk

Newlands Adventure Centre
Keswick CA12 5UF
www.activity-centre.com

Real Adventure
Kendal LA8 9DS
www.real-adventure.co.uk

River Deep Mountain High
nr Ulverston LA12 8EB
www.riverdeepmountainhigh.co.uk

Rookin House Farm
Ullswater CA11 0SS
www.rookinhouse.co.uk

Summit Treks
Coniston LA21 8DU
www.summitreks.co.uk

The Boat House
Hawkshead
Ambleside LA22 0QF
www.hawksheadtrout.com

Tree Top Trek is a high ropes course at Brockhole
www.treetoptrek.co.uk

West Lakes Adventure
Eskdale CA19 1TH
www.westlakesadventure.co.uk

Windermere Canoe Kayak
Bowness, Ambleside and Fell Foot
www.windermerecanoekayak.com

Windermere Outdoor Adventure Centre
LA23 1BP www.better.org.uk

Appendix E
Useful contacts

Tourist Information
www.golakes.co.uk and
www.lakedistrict.gov.uk
cover the whole national park.

Ambleside
LA22 9BS
0844 225 0544
tic@thehubofambleside.com

Bowness-on-Windermere
LA23 3HJ
0845 9010845
bownesstic@lakedistrict.gov.uk

Cockermouth
CA13 9NP
01900 822634

Coniston
LA21 8EH
01539 441533
mail@conistontic.org

Keswick
CA12 5JR
0845 9010845

Ullswater
CA11 0PD
017684 82414

Transport

Trains
National Rail Enquiries
0845 748 4950
www.nationalrail.co.uk

Buses
Stagecoach Cumbria
www.stagecoachbus.com

Accommodation
The following websites may be helpful:

www.lakedistrict.gov.uk
www.nationaltrust.org.uk
www.visitcumbria.com

Hostels
www.yha.org.uk

www.independenthostels.co.uk

Camping
www.pitchup.com

www.campsites.co.uk

www.campingandcaravanningclub.co.uk

Cottages
www.cumbrian-cottages.co.uk

www.lakelandcottages.co.uk

Weather
www.metoffice.gov.uk
www.mwis.org.uk
www.lakedistrictweatherline.co.uk

Notes

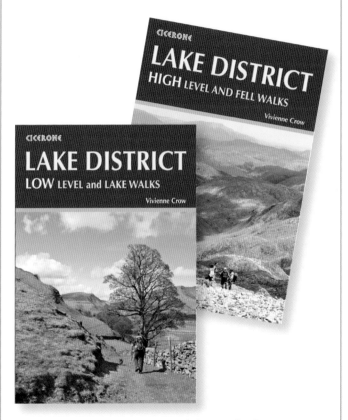

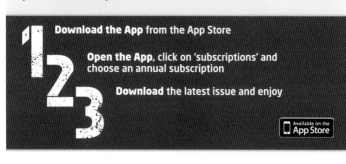

Listing of Cicerone Guides

DERBYSHIRE, PEAK DISTRICT AND MIDLANDS

Cycling in the Peak District
Dark Peak Walks
Scrambles in the Dark Peak
Walking in Derbyshire
White Peak Walks:
    The Northern Dales
White Peak Walks:
    The Southern Dales

SOUTHERN ENGLAND

20 Classic Sportive Rides in
    South East England
20 Classic Sportive Rides in
    South West England
Cycling in the Cotswolds
Mountain Biking on the
    North Downs
Mountain Biking on the
    South Downs
North Downs Way Map Booklet
South West Coast Path
    Map Booklet –
    Vol 1: Minehead to St Ives
South West Coast Path
    Map Booklet –
    Vol 2: St Ives to Plymouth
South West Coast Path
    Map Booklet –
    Vol 3: Plymouth to Poole
Suffolk Coast and Heath Walks
The Cotswold Way
The Cotswold Way Map Booklet
The Great Stones Way
The Kennet and Avon Canal
The Lea Valley Walk
The North Downs Way
The Peddars Way and Norfolk
    Coast path
The Pilgrims' Way
The Ridgeway Map Booklet
The Ridgeway National Trail
The South Downs Way
The South Downs Way
    Map Booklet
The South West Coast Path
The Thames Path
The Thames Path Map Booklet
The Two Moors Way
Two Moors Way Map Booklet
Walking Hampshire's Test Way
Walking in Cornwall
Walking in Essex
Walking in Kent
Walking in London
Walking in Norfolk
Walking in Sussex
Walking in the Chilterns
Walking in the Cotswolds
Walking in the Isles of Scilly
Walking in the New Forest

Walking in the North
    Wessex Downs
Walking in the Thames Valley
Walking on Dartmoor
Walking on Guernsey
Walking on Jersey
Walking on the Isle of Wight
Walking the Jurassic Coast
Walks in the South Downs
    National Park

BRITISH ISLES CHALLENGES, COLLECTIONS AND ACTIVITIES

The Book of the Bivvy
The Book of the Bothy
The C2C Cycle Route
The End to End Cycle Route
The Mountains of England and
    Wales: Vol 1 Wales
The Mountains of England and
    Wales: Vol 2 England
The National Trails
The UK's County Tops
Three Peaks, Ten Tors

ALPS CROSS-BORDER ROUTES

100 Hut Walks in the Alps
Across the Eastern Alps: E5
Alpine Ski Mountaineering
    Vol 1 – Western Alps
Alpine Ski Mountaineering
    Vol 2 – Central and Eastern Alps
Chamonix to Zermatt
The Karnischer Hohenweg
The Tour of the Bernina
Tour of Mont Blanc
Tour of Monte Rosa
Tour of the Matterhorn
Trail Running – Chamonix and the
    Mont Blanc region
Trekking in the Alps
Trekking in the Silvretta and
    Rätikon Alps
Trekking Munich to Venice
Walking in the Alps

PYRENEES AND FRANCE/SPAIN CROSS-BORDER ROUTES

The GR10 Trail
The GR11 Trail
The Pyrenean Haute Route
The Pyrenees
The Way of St James – Spain
Walks and Climbs in the Pyrenees

AUSTRIA

Innsbruck Mountain Adventures
The Adlerweg
Trekking in Austria's Hohe Tauern
Trekking in the Stubai Alps
Trekking in the Zillertal Alps
Walking in Austria

SWITZERLAND

Cycle Touring in Switzerland
Switzerland's Jura Crest Trail
The Swiss Alpine Pass Route –
    Via Alpina Route 1
The Swiss Alps
Tour of the Jungfrau Region
Walking in the Bernese Oberland
Walking in the Valais

FRANCE AND BELGIUM

Chamonix Mountain Adventures
Cycle Touring in France
Cycling London to Paris
Cycling the Canal de la Garonne
Cycling the Canal du Midi
Écrins National Park
Mont Blanc Walks
Mountain Adventures in
    the Maurienne
The GR20 Corsica
The GR5 Trail
The GR5 Trail – Vosges and Jura
The Grand Traverse of the
    Massif Central
The Loire Cycle Route
The Moselle Cycle Route
The River Rhone Cycle Route
The Robert Louis Stevenson Trail
The Way of St James – Le Puy
    to the Pyrenees
Tour of the Oisans: The GR54
Tour of the Queyras
Vanoise Ski Touring
Via Ferratas of the French Alps
Walking in Corsica
Walking in Provence – East
Walking in Provence – West
Walking in the Auvergne
Walking in the Briançonnais
Walking in the Cevennes
Walking in the Dordogne
Walking in the Haute Savoie:
    North
Walking in the Haute Savoie:
    South
Walks in the Cathar Region
The GR5 Trail – Benelux
    and Lorraine
Walking in the Ardennes

GERMANY

Hiking and Cycling in the
    Black Forest
The Danube Cycleway Vol 1
The Rhine Cycle Route
The Westweg
Walking in the Bavarian Alps

For full information on all our
guides, books and eBooks,
visit our website:
www.cicerone.co.uk

Walking – Trekking – Mountaineering – Climbing – Cycling

Over 40 years, Cicerone have built up an outstanding collection of over 300 guides, inspiring all sorts of amazing adventures.

Every guide comes from extensive exploration and research by our expert authors, all with a passion for their subjects. They are frequently praised, endorsed and used by clubs, instructors and outdoor organisations.

All our titles can now be bought as **e-books**, **ePubs** and **Kindle** files and we also have an online magazine – **Cicerone Extra** – with features to help cyclists, climbers, walkers and trekkers choose their next adventure, at home or abroad.

Our website shows any **new information** we've had in since a book was published. Please do let us know if you find anything has changed, so that we can publish the latest details. On our **website** you'll also find great ideas and lots of detailed information about what's inside every guide and you can buy **individual routes** from many of them online.

It's easy to keep in touch with what's going on at Cicerone by getting our monthly **free e-newsletter**, which is full of offers, competitions, up-to-date information and topical articles. You can subscribe on our home page and also follow us on **Facebook** and **Twitter** or dip into our **blog**.

Cicerone – the very best guides for exploring the world.

CICERONE

Juniper House, Murley Moss, Oxenholme Road, Kendal, Cumbria LA9 7RL
Tel: 015395 62069 info@cicerone.co.uk
www.cicerone.co.uk